The Deafening Sound of Silent Tears

Caring For Life is a Christian charity founded in 1987 to provide lifelong care, support and housing for the vulnerable or homeless, enabling people to develop dignity and self-respect. Most of those we support have been afforded little respect in the past. Our principles of care are expressed in our motto, 'Sharing the Love of Jesus'. This book, written by Juliet Barker, celebrates the charity's twentieth anniversary.

The Deafening Sound of Silent Tears:

The Story of Caring For Life

Juliet Barker

First published in 2007 by the Canterbury Press Norwich
(a publishing imprint of Hymns Ancient & Modern Limited,
a registered charity)
13–17 Long Lane, London EC1A 9PN
www.scm-canterburypress.co.uk

British Library Cataloguing in Publication data

A catalogue record for this book is available
from the British Library

ISBN 978-1-85311-850-0

Typeset by Regent Typesetting, London
Printed and bound in the UK by
CPI Bookmarque, Croydon, CR0 4TD

This book is dedicated with respect, admiration, gratitude and love to the volunteers and staff of Caring For Life, many of whom I have not been able to mention by name but without whom the charity could not function.

Never a valley so deep, never a place so dark,
but when we look down, we see there the footsteps
of the Saviour who has gone before us.

C. H. Spurgeon

Contents

Foreword

by David Kingdon
Chairman of the Trustees of Caring For Life

This book by Juliet Barker was written to mark the twentieth anniversary of Caring For Life, a Christian charity that works among homeless and marginalized people of Leeds and further afield. It began when Esther Smith and Peter Parkinson became aware of the plight of young men in a care home who were obliged to leave when they reached the age of 16 and who, at that time, had very little support as care leavers.

You will be moved as you read this book. It is a remarkable account of the compassion and love of Christians reaching out to help, in very practical ways, young people who have experienced years of unimaginable abuse, physical, sexual and mental. Many of them have learning difficulties or mental health problems. Some have drifted into crime, others into homelessness or addiction. By treating them all as made in God's image and showing them the love of Jesus, the lives of many have been transformed.

In the past 20 years over 3,000 people have benefited from the Caring For Life promise that they will be looked after for life, or for as long as they want, or need, support. Most have been enabled to live independently in the community and some have been helped to find meaningful employment.

The charity also provides a wide range of therapeutic activities based at Crag House Farm, on the outskirts of Leeds, and runs two supported homes for those who need help in looking after themselves. While success cannot always be measured in statistics alone, Caring For Life has an outstanding record. Year on year over 90 per cent of those in its care have avoided re-offending or returning to homelessness.

The Deafening Sound of Silent Tears will move you to tears and to laughter, and sometimes to anger. It did me.

I heartily commend it.

David Kingdon
Chairman of Trustees
Caring For Life

Author's Preface

I was first introduced to Caring For Life in May 2004. At the time my husband was High Sheriff of West Yorkshire, an office that lasts for a year and involves, among many other duties, attendance at royal visits to the county. When HRH The Countess of Wessex came to West Yorkshire on 19 May 2004, we were invited to join her at several of the charities she was visiting that day. Our schedule was always so hectic that it was not until we were in the car on the way to Crag House Farm that I finally found time to read the briefing notes that we had been sent.

Even though I have always lived in West Yorkshire, I had never heard of Caring For Life, and what I read shocked me to the core. Included were some of the personal stories of people who had been looked after by the charity which you will find in this book. It was like reading something out of Dickens. I could not believe that in this day and age it was still possible for such unimaginable abuse to take place at all, let alone on such a scale and, even worse, in the midst of a supposedly caring and enlightened society. When I realized that I was going to have to meet some of these deeply unhappy people face to face, I can honestly say that my heart sank. How could I, blessed with all the privileges that a loving family and a good education can bestow, possibly look them in the eye? It was clearly going to be a traumatic and depressing visit.

Nothing could have been further from the truth. The first thing we saw was smiling faces; the first thing we heard was the sound of laughter. And that, really, sums up Caring For Life. A charity that literally transforms lives by offering unconditional love to people who have never been loved before and who are often difficult to love. Like the Saviour who inspires them, those who work for Caring For Life do not judge or condemn, but seek to care for those whom society rejects: the physically disabled, the mentally ill, the prostitutes, the addicts, the violent, the criminals. How many times have you and I looked away as we walked past the dirty and unpleasant-smelling men and women who sit in station fore-courts or on benches in shopping centres, rocking backwards and forwards, muttering in a vaguely threatening manner and clutching a couple of carrier bags which contain all they possess? These are the people that Caring For Life embraces and to whom they restore dignity, humanity and hope.

I defy anyone to visit Crag House Farm and not be profoundly moved by the experience. Despite the unspoken trauma and tragedy that are the reasons for its existence, the surroundings are both beautiful and peaceful, and the whole place is imbued with a spirit of grace that is almost tangible. Even over the very short time of my involvement, I have seen young people arrive at the farm, dull-eyed, grey-skinned, morose and uninterested. To see their physical transformation into vibrant, healthy beings is remarkable and it is one of life's great pleasures to be hailed by name across the farm-yard, crushed in an almighty hug, and then given all the latest news at break-neck speed by someone who had previously been unable to look you in the eye, let alone speak to you or touch you.

The spiritual change usually takes much longer, but its results are even more dramatic: hurting, selfish, angry, violent and antagonistic people become noticeably more at ease with themselves and with others, behaving more thoughtfully, generously and lovingly. Many of them will become Christians, not because they are put under pressure to do so, or because they feel they ought to, but because they have come to recognize for themselves the healing and saving power of Christ's love which so evidently sustains those who look after them. Whether or not they do come to faith, they all share in that love and benefit from the Caring For Life promise that they will be looked after for as long as they want or need. They know that they are not 'clients' of a 'service-provider', but genuinely part of the Caring For Life family.

The more I know about the work of Caring For Life, the more I admire those who carry it out: what they do is not a job but a way of life. They make themselves available 24 hours a day, seven days a week, never knowing whether the next call will simply be a request for a food parcel or a desperate cry for help from someone who is suicidal and has already taken the pills that will end life. They require endless reserves of patience, energy and, I believe, courage to do what they do. Yet they do it (for the most part!) joyfully and with a gentleness and good humour that is inspirational to see. It seems to me that the people who work for Caring For Life – the many volunteers, the staff, and above all the two people on whom its foundation rests, Peter Parkinson and Esther Smith – truly live the gospel on a daily basis. Their faith and their commitment to those in their care are inspirational to behold. They are also a reproach to the rest of us, especially to those of us who profess to be Christians, because this is what we should all be doing. They will say that they do it for Christ, and through him, and that the glory is his. To which I say 'amen', but I also know that I am not worthy so much as to gather up the crumbs under the table of these remarkable people, to whom I humbly dedicate this book.

Juliet Barker

January 2007

Introduction

This book contains shocking stories of abuse. Most of these have come from the victims of that abuse but, wherever possible, they have also been confirmed by other sources. Readers should be aware, however, that some stories are too terrible to be told and that, in the interests of the privacy and dignity of the people concerned, significant details have been withheld. For the same reason, some names have also been changed, but these have not been identified in order to avoid drawing attention to them. Most of the names, however, are genuinely those of some of the several thousand men and women who have been helped by Caring For Life. They have given their consent for their stories to be told in this book in the hope of helping others who have been, or are, in similar situations. Many of them remain deeply damaged and vulnerable. They do not wish to discuss, or elaborate on, their personal experiences in any other context. I know that supporters of Caring For Life already understand the importance of respecting the privacy of each individual in the charity's care: I would ask that other readers also extend the same courtesy. Any legitimate enquiries should be addressed directly to Caring For Life.

I am deeply grateful to those looked after by the charity who have allowed their stories to be told: I admire their courage and their honesty. In addition, I would like to thank the many members of staff, volunteers and supporters who have contributed their own memories and anecdotes of the last 20 years. Like the many individuals, companies and grant-making trusts who have supported the charity over the same period, they are too numerous to mention by name, but their contributions have been, and remain, immensely valued and vital to the continuation of the work.

Caring For Life has given me access to its archive, which includes contemporary newsletters and bulletins to supporters, newspaper cuttings, minute books and photographic material. I have drawn heavily on these sources, particularly the bulletins, to reconstruct the charity's history and to find the personal stories of those involved. I am also indebted to Peter Parkinson and Esther Smith who have read several drafts of this book and corrected many errors. They had intended to write this book themselves, but I thought that this would be a distraction from their work, which is infinitely more important. I therefore offered to write the book for them and I hope that what follows is a fair reflection of a remarkable story told, as I was requested to do, 'warts and all'.

1

The Lost Boys

On 28 February 1987 Peter Parkinson, the pastor of Leeds Reformed Baptist Church, set out on a mission that was to change not only his life but also the lives of all around him. He was going to collect the four young men who were to be the first residents of Caring For Life, a new charity for homeless young people, which had been formed only a few weeks earlier. A supporter had offered the use of an empty property he owned in Yeadon, a pleasant town on the outskirts of Leeds in West Yorkshire, and a frenetic 48 hours had been spent finding furniture, a fridge, a cooker and all the other basic amenities that would turn the house into a home. When the young men arrived, Carey House would be fully furnished, warm and welcoming, with tea waiting for them on the table. For the first time in their lives they would have a home of their own; more significantly, they had the promise that they would have a home for life.

Suburban, ordinary and safe, Carey House was everything that these young men had never experienced before. Two of them had spent many years in institutions. Owen had grown up in local authority care, was unable to read or write, and was struggling to break away from his family, some of whom were notorious local criminals. Gary had learning difficulties which had made him vulnerable to abuse from childhood – abuse that had continued when he was sent away at the age of 12 to a special residential school. Easily exploited and living alone but unable to look after himself properly, he was in acute danger. Colin had been physically and emotionally neglected throughout his childhood because of his father's serious psychiatric illness; malnourished and confused, he was desperate for proper care. William's life had fallen apart when he was just 14. One day he had returned home from school to find that both his parents were dead. His mother, who had fought a long battle against cancer, was lying in bed, and at her feet hung the body of his father, who had committed suicide. William was taken in by his sister, but he was not allowed to join her family in the house; instead he had to live in an outbuilding in her backyard where his only supply of water was the toilet. He had never gone back to school and, when Peter picked him up, he was still wearing the same clothes that he had been wearing on the day his parents died. He was in urgent need of medical treatment – an observer commented that he walked like an old man due to the pain in his feet which were covered in verrucas – and he was so severely traumatized by his experiences that he was virtually unable to speak.

Tragic though these individual stories were, they were by no means unique, but simply variations on a theme that was only just coming to public attention. Prior to the mid-1980s, most homeless people were aged over 30 and many had lived on the streets for a long time. That profile was changing dramatically, and by the end of the decade the large night shelters and hostels intended as temporary accommodation for often elderly 'vagrants' were filling with young people, most of them aged between 16 and 21. There was a number of reasons for this: the spiralling rise in divorce rates and family breakdowns, which had resulted in many more one-parent and step-families, where abuse is statistically more likely to occur; a revolution in child protection work, which had heightened awareness of the sexual abuse of children and, through widespread media coverage, had encouraged young people to exercise their right to leave abusive situations; and changes in the benefit system for the under-18s, combined with a lack of local authority housing stock, which made it increasingly difficult to re-house the young homeless.

Another factor, which was of particular relevance to the situation in a large city like Leeds, was that until the Children Act of 1989 there was no legal obligation to provide leaving care or support beyond the age of 16, and therefore many vulnerable young people who had spent years in children's homes suddenly found themselves thrown entirely on their own resources.[1] Mari Piper, who was put into care in Cumbria at the age of 12, spent the next five years moving 30 times across five different regions, living in five children's homes, and having 20 different sets of foster parents. Looking back

---

1 Over 20 years later it is scandalous that such neglect can still occur, despite the reforms of the Children Act and subsequent legislation.

on that time, she movingly summed up the problems she had faced:

> In care, someone is controlling what you eat, where you go and when you go out. It's not a normal home. To have to ask someone if you can make a cup of tea, to get written permission for new socks (and then a receipt when you buy them), to never have space for yourself, even to never be sure the bed you wake up in is going to be the same one that night, is really horrible . . . Then at 16 or 17 you're told 'there's your flat'. From having no control, suddenly you've got all of it. And quite often it's when you're stressed doing GCSEs or A Levels, which is not the best time. Some people haven't learnt to cook, and where do you pay your gas bill? How do you claim council tax relief? How do you register with a doctor or a dentist?[2]

Without the necessary skills to manage independent living, many of those who had outgrown council care fell into debt or failed to pay their rents, and were swiftly evicted by their landlords. 'Seventeen, on benefit, ex-care, trying to find a flat is very difficult.'[3] Many of them inevitably became homeless. This brought problems of a different kind: never knowing where you will sleep tonight or tomorrow night; living out of carrier bags – and having to carry them round with you; feeling rejected by everyone – family, friends, the care system,

---

2 *Yorkshire Evening Post*, 28 April 1999.
3 Ibid.

people who pass you by on the streets; dreading every move, whether to an unfriendly hostel or to a dingy, lonely bed-sit; living in fear of being assaulted and having to stay half-awake as you sleep on the streets; feeling labelled as a scrounger, a junkie, a criminal. And without a home address, employment was virtually impossible to find. Unable to cope, and often haunted by traumatic personal problems from their past, it was not surprising that these young people often began the slide into criminal activity, drug and alcohol abuse, self-harm and, all too frequently, suicide.

It was a growing awareness of the problems facing those leaving care that inspired the foundation of Caring For Life. Peter Parkinson had always chosen to exercise his calling in the most difficult and deprived areas of northern England. As a student pastor in theological college, his ministry had been in the notorious Moss Side area of Manchester and then he had worked on the equally crime- and drug-ridden estates of Harehills and Chapeltown in Leeds. As the founding pastor of Leeds Reformed Baptist Church, Peter had continued to encourage a very active social ministry into the local community, particularly among the university students who lived in the Headingley area. One of those students, Esther Smith, had become a member of the church while taking a degree in Hebrew and Theology. After graduating, she obtained employment with the Leeds Department of Social Services and, in 1979, she was appointed housemother in charge of Foxcroft Children's Home, a local authority home in Headingley. Her principal assistant, Wendy Pollard, was also a committed Christian and a member of the same church.

'Between them they made Foxcroft a special place,' Peter Parkinson remembered at Wendy's funeral in 1999:

> Rarely, if ever, could you find a local authority children's home which worked so wonderfully, and so consistently, in the interests of the children, as Esther and Wendy achieved at Foxcroft . . . their consistent compassion for every aspect of the children's welfare, including their spiritual welfare, bore tremendous fruits.

Putting the children's welfare first sometimes involved difficult decisions that brought conflict with the Department of Social Services. Esther was ahead of her time, for example, in insisting that siblings should be kept together, rather than divided between different foster parents and carers. Similarly, she fought against the policy that allowed children in care to be sent home for the weekend, because she knew from experience that this often meant that they were being returned to their abusers.

As a result, those who were fortunate enough to live at Foxcroft during the 13 years that Esther and Wendy were in charge were 'extraordinarily free from the scars that so many children suffer when experiencing local authority "care"'. Many of them would later describe how they felt safe there – cared for, looked after and protected – in a way that some of them had not experienced before or since.

The happy atmosphere at Foxcroft also owed much to the involvement of Peter Parkinson, who was an official visitor to the home.[4] Always ready to talk to the children, listen to them and play with them, he built up their trust and provided some of them with the first contact with a safe paternal figure that they had ever experienced. Peter still recalls his shock, revulsion and pity when one little girl, just three or four years old, sat on his knee, lifted her skirt and casually told him 'to get on with it'. When he asked her what she meant, she said 'let's get it over with now, Uncle Peter, and then we can play'. Such was her experience of childhood that she expected sexual abuse to be the price she had to pay for the privilege of playing with an adult.

The plight of children like these, who had never known innocence or unconditional love, had a profound impact on Peter, not least because he was himself the father of two small boys, the elder of whom was the same age as most of those at Foxcroft. And as a Christian minister, whose life was committed to sharing the love of Jesus with others and following his example, he could not ignore Jesus' commandment that 'he who believes in me will also do the works that I do'.[5] It was not enough for him simply to pay his duty visits to the home: like Esther and Wendy, he wanted to reclaim these children's childhood and show them that, however bad their experiences in the past had been, they were still precious in the sight of God.

---

4 Two other people who were involved in Caring For Life from its inception, Russell Bridges, the assistant pastor of Leeds Reformed Baptist Church, and Rod Wark, a police officer, were also official visitors at the home.

5 John 14.12.

Peter and his wife, Judith, therefore, obtained permission to invite the Foxcroft children into their own home, and their two young sons, Jonathan and Tim, grew up in the midst of an extended family of boys and girls who, in the ordinary walk of life, would rarely have crossed their paths. While some children might have resented having to share their parents' time and affection, it was a situation that Jonathan and Tim accepted without question or reservation. Most of the children were the same age as Jonathan:

> These guys were an extension to our family. I knew my dad loved me, but I knew that he wanted them to know his love too. I believe that God honours those who honour him and these children needed love and they needed friends who would accept them for who they were, warts and all, and the great bonus for me was that they also accepted me with all my faults. Having to share your dad with lots of other people was sometimes hard, but it was never hard to share him with Esther's children.

> In terms of my relationship with the kids at Foxcroft, they were quite simply my best and closest friends. I never looked down on them or thought they were different because they lived in a home, but it was obvious even to me at a very young age that some of my friends could be a little bit unpredictable. Often some of them would be angry, sad, destructive, but on the other hand they could also be great fun and funny; sometimes they were quiet and introverted, obviously struggling with something, but then again the same person could be an extrovert. I learnt

quickly that there were times when I had to be careful what I said and did but, at the same time, I would have to continue to be me – their friend – who did care for them.

For Tim, too:

> These people were my playmates. Friends. They just lived together. It didn't really cross my mind that they didn't have a 'normal' family with a mum and dad at home. I think I just accepted them as I saw them. A family of their own, with Esther and Wendy as their mums and my dad as the person they looked up to as their dad.

The fact that Tim was three years younger than both his brother and most of the Foxcroft children gave him a slightly different perspective. The age difference put him in the position of being the outsider who sought acceptance from the group. Though he did not realize it at the time, this gave him a valuable insight into those whose lives were blighted because they were seen as being different:

> Maybe my view on this is wrong but I think – looking back now – they came from broken homes. They had been rejected, abused, and more. And they, I am sure, would have longed to be accepted and treated as normal. But for me . . . I wanted to be the one who was accepted by *them*. I wanted their acceptance as being one of the group. I wanted to be part of that special family. And I was the privileged one who was allowed to play with these guys and girls whom others had treated so differently from the way that they

should have been. I really didn't know what or where they had come from but, for me, at that stage, it didn't matter. What mattered was that they would like me.

Whether it was sharing mealtimes (and trying to avoid clearing up afterwards), hiding around the house, having raucous mock fights, playing space invader games or simply running round the racetrack at Carnegie College, the Parkinson boys spent many hours in the company of these friends. Together they attended the church Sunday School and the older ones also went on the church camps to Wales. They became familiar members of the congregation, though their presence was not always without incident. Young people who have suffered serious abuse and have many difficulties and are often illiterate cannot be expected to behave like the average church member. (One former Foxcroft resident recalls how he thought Sunday School was a big joke and he would do silly things such as standing on a bench and copying the minister by raising his hands in the air as if in prayer.) Inevitably, services were occasionally disrupted and some level of offence was caused, but the reaction was usually both tolerant and compassionate.

It was not surprising, therefore, that it was to Leeds Reformed Baptist Church that some of these people turned when they had nowhere else to go. In the latter part of 1986 a group of seven homeless young men began to attend the church, drawn back by a desperate need for friendship to the only individuals who had ever shown them love and care in childhood. Some of them had been residents at Foxcroft; others had only attended the Sunday School. Since then they had all struggled to support themselves. They lacked the abilities or skills to find and keep employment or accommodation, and did not have family or friends to fall back on for either financial or emotional support.

This was a major challenge to anyone, let alone a group of Christians who professed to follow the Saviour who had preached the parable of the good Samaritan. The dilemma was obvious, but the solution was not. Clearly they could not turn away and walk by on the other side completely, but was it enough simply to take a caring interest in the young men, give them Bibles, and encourage them to come to church each Sunday? Or should they do as Jesus himself had done and take up a compassionate and practical ministry towards the poor? In an ideal world the answer was as obvious as the dilemma. They should roll up their sleeves and get stuck into the tough, exacting and sometimes unsavoury task of helping the young people in a very practical and down-to-earth way, seeking to love them as Jesus loved us and to share the gospel with them. But there were risks in doing this. It would require an enormous commitment of time, money and effort by people who had little enough to spare because they were already leading busy lives of their own. There was also the danger that it might become a purely social mission without any spiritual dimension: provision for the body, but not for the soul.

There was, not surprisingly, a natural reluctance to engage personally with the problem. Both Peter and Esther remember one heated exchange at the time. Peter had said, 'Somebody ought to do something about this!', to which she had replied, 'Well, what are *you* going to do about it?' 'What can *I* do?' was Peter's all too human response. 'Everyone says that,' Esther scolded him, 'but we can do something, no matter how small. If all of us do something, then it will make a difference, no matter how small.'

It was a challenge that could not be ignored, particularly by those who had known some of the individuals from childhood. Although Leeds Reformed Baptist Church had a very active social outreach programme, the nature of this particular problem was such that it would be impractical to expect every decision to be taken by a church meeting. Instead, it was decided to set up a registered charity, with several members of the church as its trustees. At the inaugural meeting, on 18 January 1987, Peter Parkinson was appointed chairman; his wife Judith, secretary; and Owen Carey-Jones, treasurer. The other trustees present were Peter's assistant pastor, Russell Bridges, the two ladies who ran Foxcroft Children's Home, Esther Smith and Wendy Pollard, and Barbara Beevers, a sympathetic member of Leeds Reformed Baptist Church. The charity would operate on the principle that every human being is made in the image of God and, as the object of his love, should be treated with dignity and respect. It would bring to the people in its care the same love and compassion that Christ had shown to mankind and offer relief to those in need, especially the homeless and the vulnerable. The name of the charity, Caring For Life, was carefully chosen to reflect its purpose and intention: care would be offered to all for life, or for as long as it was wanted, rather than just for the short-term.

This was particularly ambitious, since the new charity had

neither money nor property, only a determination to find both and an absolute conviction that God would provide – and he did. Owen Carey-Jones's job was relocated to a different part of the country, but he had not sold his house in Rufford Drive, Yeadon. He therefore generously offered to loan it to the charity to provide a home for four young men. It would be named Carey House, after the missionary William Carey, whose inspiring words 'Expect great things *from* God and attempt great things *for* God' were so relevant to the aspirations of Caring For Life.

There was now no hesitation or holding back. Church members volunteered to help furnish it and to assist in its running. Christian magazines and other churches were contacted to raise much-needed funds for its support. The seven young men whose plight had prompted the foundation of Caring For Life were informed of the intention to open the home and the news spread rapidly. Within three weeks more than 80 applications had been received for the four places. The extent of the need for homes for young people was clearly far greater than anyone had thought.

Peter and his fellow trustees were equally naïve in making their preparations to welcome the first residents of Caring For Life. Expecting them to come laden with all the usual paraphernalia of teenage life, Peter had hired a three-ton box van to collect their belongings and bring them back to Carey House. To his embarrassment, he discovered that everything each young man owned could be carried away in one or two carrier bags. The full realization of how destitute these young men were did not fully dawn until a few days later, when one of them, who had refused to be parted from his bag or allow anyone to look into it, broke down in tears. He had been too ashamed to admit that he possessed nothing at all, except the clothes that he stood up in, and had tried to hide the fact by filling his bag with bricks and old newspapers.

The young men who were welcomed to Carey House that February night could not have imagined how their lives would change. Nervous at first, they could not hide their astonishment and joy when they were invited to choose a room of their own. Most of them had never enjoyed that privilege before. And that evening, for the first but not the last time, the sound of laughter rang round the house as skinny young men who had no nightwear of their own came sheepishly down to supper wearing pyjamas borrowed from Peter which they had had to tie up with string. The clothes that they had arrived in were washed – and some of them were so worn that they promptly disintegrated in the washing machine. Over the next few days and weeks, new clothes and shoes had to be purchased: one young man proudly informed the shop assistant that he had never had proper shoes before, but that now he was living at Caring For Life he had a pair for work *and* a pair for best.

A rota of unpaid volunteers, mostly members of Leeds Reformed Baptist Church, took turns to stay overnight in Carey House, providing security, supervision and assistance whenever needed. From the very beginning, however, it was always emphasized that this was a home, not an institution. As a visitor to one of the later houses remarked, 'It doesn't look like a hostel. It doesn't smell like a hostel. It's just like walking into anyone's home.' Achieving this meant that there was much for the young men to learn. 'I remember having to teach some basic hygiene,' Barbara Beevers recalls, 'for example, you don't wash the pots up with a dishcloth and then use the same cloth to clean your shoes!'

More importantly, it meant instilling into the young men the idea that they each had a right to personal privacy, but that they also had a duty to respect it in others. This was a totally alien concept to most of them. Their lives had been spent amid chaotic and dysfunctional families or in institutions where anyone, particularly an authority figure, could intrude at will, even in the most intimate situations. At Caring For Life they were given the dignity of controlling their own lives: no one was allowed to enter the house, or their rooms, without their permission – visitors were invited guests. Learning to trust each other did not come so easily. One new arrival always took his belongings out with him in plastic bags when he left his room for the day, unable to believe that his few treasured possessions would still be there when he returned.

At the same time as Carey House was opening its doors to its first residents, Caring For Life was also embarking on another even more ambitious project. Overwhelmed by the number of applicants for places, the trustees had approached Leeds City Council in the hope that more accommodation could be found. Two adjoining properties in Meanwood were identified as a potential new home, but there were serious drawbacks. The buildings were on an estate scheduled for demolition and they were in a very dilapidated state.

Unlike leafy and respectable suburban Yeadon, Meanwood in the 1980s was a deprived inner-city area with many social problems and high crime rates. Nevertheless, the council was prepared to offer the two properties to Caring For Life as a loan for a period of three years. It was an opportunity that could not be missed. Friends, supporters and well-wishers all offered their services, and work began on restoring the houses to make them habitable again.

It was at this point that a remarkable young man named Tony Tindall was drawn into the project. Tony was just 20 and was suffering from terminal cancer. A mere 12 months earlier he had been a carefree teenager with a penchant for Aikido, heavy metal music, night clubs and girls, so the diagnosis had come as a terrible shock. Constant pain and the side-effects of powerful doses of chemotherapy and radiotherapy had left him feeling lost, isolated and fearful in the face of approaching death. In this vulnerable state, he had been approached by members of the Charismatic Movement who promised him a miraculous cure. 'I wanted them to be right – so very much,' Tony later confessed, so he went to their faith-healing groups where various ministers had spoken in tongues and laid their hands on him, but he had not got better and the tumour in his pelvis had continued to grow. When he dared to question why, he was told that it was only his lack of faith that prevented his being healed.

Despite this experience, Tony had actually come to faith himself through reading his Bible and he was determined to make the most of the short time he had left by taking up charitable work. In February 1987, he was introduced to

Caring For Life by Bob Johns, a local policeman whom he had met in hospital. He struck up an immediate rapport with Peter Parkinson, was baptized, and became a member of his church. 'To be able to visit friends in the church, do evangelistic work and help Peter with Caring For Life gave me some of the happiest times of my life,' he wrote later:

> It was a very exciting time to be involved: I used my car for transportation jobs and running errands; I helped with the decorating of the houses; I befriended the boys who would be moving in, and eventually helped them settle in. My father, who is an electrician, completely re-wired one of the houses . . . Thus began an association with a pastor and people that was to be a source of strength and hope during the months ahead . . . they helped me to see that I could work for God now; that my life was not over, but during the remaining time I could live and speak for Him, and this I wanted to do more than anything.[6]

Tony's contribution towards setting up the new home had been so important that the trustees determined to name it after him. Tindall House officially opened in July 1987, just five months after Carey House and seven months before Tony died. Carol Raettig, who had been the first residential member of staff at Carey House while on weekends off from her employment in Rutland, moved to the new home and started

---

6 Vivienne Wood, *Tony* (Mayflower Christian Books, 1988), pp. 44–7. Tony died on 2 March 1988, just two months after his twenty-first birthday.

working full time for Caring For Life. Moving into Tindall House proved to be a real learning experience not only for her but also for the young men, who were all involved in the renovation, redecoration and furnishing. On one occasion, they were startled by the arrival of the police. One of the boys, who was well known to them as a petty burglar, had been spotted up a ladder and they thought he was trying to force an entry. It fell to Carol to calm a fraught situation and explain that, for once in his life, he was doing something he was supposed to be doing: he was actually puttying in the window.

Living on the estate could be difficult and sometimes dangerous, especially for female members of staff. One supervisor, Dee Hewitt, was threatened by a lad on the estate and later received several unpleasant telephone calls. Carol recalls, however, that:

> The lads and I developed a respect for each other and they were very protective of me. I remember a time when a couple came to the door being very abusive and threatening, but eventually they backed off. I thought it was the force of my personality that had won the argument – but turned round to find that five of the lads were standing menacingly behind me.

The young men were all expected to take their share of the household chores, learning, under supervision, the basic skills of cooking, cleaning and shopping which would, hopefully, one day help to give them a degree of independence:

One evening one of the lads decided to prepare a curry. I gave instructions on how to cook it but he wouldn't believe a couple of teaspoons of curry powder would do the trick. It was the hottest curry I've ever eaten before or since. Nobody criticized the meal, but he certainly learned his lesson. Unfortunately we had two visitors staying to tea who were interested in the work of Caring For Life. We never did see or hear from them again.

One of the earliest residents of Tindall House was Antony. He arrived at Caring For Life in January 1988, handcuffed to two police officers who described him as a prolific petty offender, violent and unable to speak. Had he not been accepted into Caring For Life's care 24 hours a day, he would have had to serve a long prison sentence. Some 16 years later – and still living at Tindall House – he described in his own words what his previous life had been:

I was born in Bristol, but I have lived in Leeds since I was five months old. Before I was a Christian I was not happy, and I had no friends at all. When I was little, many bad things happened to me. I don't ever remember a time as a child when bad things did not happen to me ... I never asked God to help me when bad things happened. I didn't think there could be a God, because, if there was, he wouldn't have let those bad things happen to me that did happen.

My sister is a Christian, and she had bad things done to her as well. She says that when bad things used to happen to me, she would pray for me. She is really poorly now, and sometimes hears my father's voice. It was my father who did the bad things to us.

Until I became a Christian the happiest day in my life was the day I heard that my father was dead. That was because he was the person who made us all suffer so much, and who did bad things to us, and now he was dead. I was glad when I heard that he was dead. But I still didn't have any friends.

When I was six, I was sent away to boarding school from Monday to Friday. It was better than home, but I hated it and kept running away. At school they always made me do things that weren't nice. I often would just walk around town all night and sleep on the benches in the railway station. The police would pick me up and send me back to the school.

At 16 I left school and just stayed home. I didn't do much during the day – I just stopped in. Sometimes I would go to the local betting shop to back horses. I was moved to a children's home, but I hated it very much. I was always running away. One time I stayed away for two weeks over Christmas and New Year. It was very cold and I got very hungry wandering the streets.

For many months after his arrival at Caring For Life, Antony would not speak at all or even look anyone in the eye. He shied away from all physical contact and trembled with fear if anyone spoke loudly near him or made a sudden movement. Once he did begin to talk, he revealed the terrible history of childhood abuse to which he alludes in his own account. His father had subjected him to such vicious physical abuse that Antony would literally pass out when he came near him. As happened so often with those taken into care at this period, the abuse had continued at both his children's homes and at boarding school. His vulnerability had been compounded by the fact that he suffered from Asperger's Syndrome, a form of autism, which made it difficult for him to communicate with and relate to others. Although he showed all the classic symptoms, including an obsessive interest in learning facts and figures, a dependence on routine and an inability to socialize appropriately, the diagnosis had been missed in childhood, so nothing had been done to help him develop the basic skills that would have made his life easier. Building those skills and, more importantly, his trust, would take many years of patient loving care.[7]

---

7 For information on autism and Asperger's Syndrome, see the National Autistic Society website www.nas.org.uk.

2

Crag House Farm: The Heart of Caring For Life

For Antony, as for many other young people in Caring For Life's care, rescue came not just from finding a permanent and loving home – critically important though that was – but from working at Crag House Farm.

West Yorkshire has many pockets of green amid its urban and industrial landscape, and the farm occupies one of them. It stands on a windy hilltop at Cookridge, a small town on the outskirts of Leeds. Although it is close to the city – and Leeds Bradford airport is just across the valley – it is remarkably rural and peaceful. The implementation of a series of conservation schemes over the years has now also turned it into a haven for wildlife and a place of exceptional beauty.

Crag House Farm was an inspired choice for what would become the heart of Caring For Life because for centuries it had been a place of both work and prayer. It was built on lands that had once belonged to the Cistercian Abbey at Kirkstall, which is now in the city of Leeds, but in the twelfth century had been an uncultivated wasteland. The Cistercians had then combined a deep spirituality with a simple, even austere, way of life. Unlike other monastic orders of the time, they did not choose to build their abbeys in towns and rely on traditional feudal sources of income, but sought instead to reclaim land from the wild by the toil of their own hands. They did not withdraw from the world, but engaged with it, devoting themselves to earning both a worldly living by working their lands and a place in heaven by prayer. It was an ethos to which Caring For Life, 900 years later, would also subscribe.

The Parkinsons had bought Crag House Farm in 1980.[8] The move had, in some ways, been forced upon them by their commitment to the boys and girls from Foxcroft Children's Home, whose regular visits to the Parkinsons' family home at Adel had not been appreciated by the neighbours. There had begun to be complaints – quite justified as the Parkinsons admit – about the noise the children made, particularly when they were playing in the garden. Rather than curtail their activities, the Parkinsons decided to look for another house that had enough open space around it to allow the children to play as boisterously as they wished, without intruding on others. Crag House Farm was ideally suited to their needs: close enough to Leeds Reformed Baptist Church and Foxcroft to maintain both ministries, but also surrounded by open fields. Although they could not afford to purchase the entire farm, they were able to scrape together enough money to buy the main farmhouse, the adjacent barns and the four fields closest to the house.

---

8 Don Cole, *Crag Farm, Cookridge, in the Ancient Parish of Adel* (1995), p. 35.

From the very beginning, Crag House Farm was not just a family home but a place of healing ministry for the disadvantaged. The Foxcroft children were regular visitors, taking particular delight in riding the ponies from the small riding school which Debbie Habibzadeh, a member of Leeds Reformed Baptist Church, ran at the farm. They were soon joined by others with special needs and learning disabilities for whom growing pot plants or looking after the hens and goats had enormous therapeutic value. The plan had originally been to run the farm as a business, ploughing all the profits back into the ministry, but it rapidly became clear that it would never generate enough money to meet the level of need.

After the foundation of Caring For Life, the young men who lived in Tindall and Carey House were expected to work at the farm every weekday, unless otherwise employed or in education or training. This remains a condition of taking up residency in one of the charity's homes, but it has caused considerable controversy, especially in recent years. It is frowned upon by some government agencies which believe that the young people should be able to choose whether they wish to work or not. However, working at the farm is central to the ethos of Caring For Life and its purpose is twofold. First, to give structure, predictability and stability to often chaotic lives: the simple routine of having to get up in the morning and go to work in a place where others depend upon you is a useful discipline and also a distraction from personal problems. For those with learning difficulties, especially those suffering from autism or Asperger's Syndrome, who have a compulsive need for order and unvarying routine, it can be the only means of keeping acute anxiety at bay.[9]

Second, working on the farm gives meaningful employment that raises self-esteem and teaches skills that can be stepping-stones to future independence. Most of the young people who have been cared for by Caring For Life have some degree of learning difficulty. This means that they are slower at processing information, their ability to learn new things without losing what they already have is limited, and their learning development has effectively stalled, usually at a very early age. From childhood, therefore, their learning experience has been invariably negative. The education system, with its emphasis on purely academic skills, is very good at identifying what children cannot do and seeks to change this by making them do more of it: if you fail a maths test, you have to take it again. For those with learning difficulties this can never be the answer: it simply reinforces the cycle of failure. In recent times, the drive towards inclusion in schools, though well-meaning, has exacerbated the problem. Instead of being labelled as 'different' by going to Special Schools, where at least their difficulties were recognized and addressed within a protected atmosphere, they are humiliated and stigmatized by being included in mainstream education where they fail publicly to meet the targets and attainments expected of their peers. The only thing they learn easily is 'I'm useless', an attitude that has repercussions for their ability to deal with daily

9 Daniel Tammet, who has Asperger's Syndrome, has given a fascinating insight into what it is like to have the condition in his book, *Born on a Blue Day* (Hodder & Stoughton, 2006).

life. As the Mencap slogan so succinctly puts it, 'Just because I don't think as fast, doesn't mean I don't feel as deeply'.

Breaking this pattern of negativity can only be achieved by recognizing the needs of each individual, focusing on what it is possible for them to achieve and celebrating every success, however small. From the outset, the work provided at Crag House Farm was intended to meet the needs of a wide range of abilities. The objectives were always to build up confidence and give the young people that sense of achievement that only comes by being involved in, and finishing, worthwhile tasks. Although the progress can often be slow and much reassurance is needed along the way, working towards and actually achieving certain goals has proved to be enormously valuable to the individuals concerned. The young people had the choice of working either in the horticultural project, growing fruits, salads and vegetables from seed to plate, and plants to sell to the local community, or in the agricultural project, collecting eggs from several thousand free-range hens and looking after rare breeds of cattle, goats and sheep. Those with autism or Asperger's, who did not necessarily relate to cuddly pets, often demonstrated an affinity for the birds of prey, which included a barn owl and a redtail hawk.

Working with animals, whose lives and health are entirely reliant upon human care, can be very rewarding to those whose own lives have been marked by continuous rejection. And animals can sometimes be the best therapists. As Joe, who helped to look after Luther the shire-horse for many years, remarked, he had told Luther many secrets over the years, 'but he has never told anyone what I told him'.

It was Antony, one of the first residents of Tindall House, however, who was perhaps the most dramatic beneficiary of God's healing through the therapeutic power of animals. For many months after his arrival at Caring For Life, Antony had refused to speak to anyone and simply shrugged his shoulders in response to any question. As he started to work at Crag House Farm, caring for the sheep and goats, he began to mimic animal sounds and it became clear that he could speak, if he chose to do so. Since Antony shunned all eye contact, Peter decided to start talking to him through the animals. He would stand a little distance away while Antony was feeding the goats, and then ask the goats how Antony was feeling. Eventually, after several weeks, Antony finally spoke. He told the goat to tell Peter that he was 'OK'. As he became more at ease, he displayed an unsuspected sense of humour. In reply to the goat being asked if there was anything Antony wanted to say, Antony replied, 'Tell him I'm fed up with all this conversation.' This breakthrough led to a gradual building of confidence so that Antony began not only to speak directly with other people at Caring For Life but also to make eye contact and even, eventually, to accept demonstrations of affection.

It was not just the young men at Tindall and Carey House who attended the farm. Its facilities were also open to all the people whom Caring For Life supported in the community. This aspect of the charity's work had not been part of the original plan, but had grown naturally out of the desire to help as many of the homeless young people who were referred to them as possible. The demand for places in the two homes would always far outstrip their availability, but Esther Smith's contacts with the Housing Department meant that she knew where and how to access local authority housing on their behalf. Sometimes, with mediation and practical assistance, it was even possible to return young people to their families. In either case, however, continuing support was needed. In some cases this meant Caring For Life staff and volunteers visiting them regularly in their own homes, helping them to organize their finances and arrange appointments with doctors and dentists, or simply providing friendship and a listening ear to people who were otherwise alone.

For many of these young people, working at Crag House Farm was an opportunity not only to learn skills that might help them find employment but also to have social and emotional engagement. The emphasis was on creating a family atmosphere in which recreation also played an important part. Epic games of football in the lunch-hour became the norm for the active, but sharing meals and even just having conversations together played as great a part in making the young people feel that they belonged to the extended Caring For Life family. The grandly titled Resource Centre, better (and more appropriately) known as 'the hut', was the focal meeting point. This was a place for Bible study for those who wished to learn more about the love of Jesus that had inspired the work of Caring For Life; a workshop where those who wanted to learn wood-working skills could make specially designed nesting boxes for different types of birds and mammals, including owls and bats; and sometimes, in the cold, wet and windy days of autumn and winter, just a place to huddle for warmth.

It was on these occasions, or when working side by side with staff and volunteers, or sometimes when simply enjoying the companionship of walking through the fields, that confidences could be shared and tales of unimaginable abuse, hidden for years, could be brought to light. One very damaged autistic boy who came regularly to the farm could be extremely violent at the home where he lived, but refused to talk to anyone at all about his problems. However, he did form a strong bond with Misty the barn owl and would walk around the farm with it, talking to it and telling it why he was upset. By listening in on these conversations, it was possible to find out what was wrong and inform his carers at the home, who were then able to help him.

At the beginning of May 1988, the trustees held a meeting to review Caring For Life's progress and, in an understated minute, recorded that 'We felt that although we had been going for just over a year, the Lord had blessed the work.' From a standing start, without money, property or experience, the charity had two homes up and running that housed 15 young men and provided day-care facilities for them at the farm. The icing on the cake was the fact that 2 of the young men in their care had become Christians. All this had been achieved at considerable personal cost, not least for the trustees themselves. Peter Parkinson had been trying to make ends meet by running a photography business as well as continuing to devote so much of his time to Leeds Reformed Baptist Church and Caring For Life; his wife Judith, a pivotal figure at the charity, despite her preference for being in the background, was working as an Avon lady, in addition to looking after both her two boys and also a member of the church with severe emotional and psychological problems who was in need of constant care; Esther Smith was holding down a demanding job at Foxcroft, but also getting up early each morning to milk the goats before she set off for work, and then spending her weekends as the residential supervisor at one or other of Caring For Life's homes. It was not a situation that could continue indefinitely but, buoyed up by their success, the trustees were determined to expand the charity's remit.

At the same meeting they set down their ambitious priorities for the next 12 months: to find a replacement home for Tindall House, to set up two further new homes, including one for sexually abused girls, and to provide sheltered accommodation for those who had outgrown the 24-hour care provided by Caring For Life but were not capable of independent living in the community. It would be many years before these goals were achieved – and the dream to provide sheltered accommodation remains alive, but unrealized, to this day. Two important decisions were taken, however, which would enable what had begun as a voluntary organization to become more professional. Caring For Life needed a proper administrative base and the obvious place was Crag House Farm which could also have a vital role providing the pastoral environment for work experience, counselling and recreation. Through the generosity of the Parkinson family, including Peter's mother, 'Aunty Lily', who had also helped purchase the property, Crag House Farm was transferred in early 1989 to CFL Properties, a company controlled by the charity. Loyal supporters helped finance the move by subscribing for shares in the company. And Esther Smith agreed that she would become the trust's full-time senior administrator, with special pastoral responsibilities; Wendy Pollard, too, would later join the staff, taking over as resident supervisor of Tindall House.

On 18 March 1989 Caring For Life hosted its first official Open Day at Crag House Farm. Visitors and supporters were able to see rare breeds of cattle, goats and poultry, Tamworth pigs, Hebridean sheep, a shire-horse, ponies, geese and cashmere rabbits, all of which had been given to the farm by friends of the charity. The concentration on rare breeds was part of a deliberate conservation policy which at that time was unusual, but reflected Caring For Life's commitment to the preservation of every aspect of God's creation, not just those made in his own image. Caring for nature involved tree planting, protecting wild flowers, establishing a butterfly garden and providing nesting sites for birds. The development of the herb garden, with over a hundred varieties of herb (planted by Esther in 1988, 'and I haven't had time to weed it since!'), together with the growing of fresh vegetables and fruit, were also steps on the way to self-sufficiency. At this time the main source of income was the sale of free-range eggs which were collected, graded and boxed for local supermarkets, but the potential for all these other projects to expand was enormous. All that was missing was time and money.

These were in increasingly short supply as the Caring For Life success story became more widely known. The rate of referrals from Social Services was increasing exponentially. In July 1989 the government drastically reduced the amount of money payable to young people in bed-and-breakfast accommodation, leaving many unable to pay their landlords and therefore becoming homeless. Three months later Caring For Life had a waiting list of at least 25 'desperate' cases needing accommodation and no vacant places to offer them. The situation was replicated in many parts of the UK, and members of other independent churches, particularly those in the Grace Baptist tradition, were pressing the charity to launch similar projects in their communities.

Convinced that it would be possible to roll out their model countrywide, the trustees put much time and effort into setting up various initiatives under the Caring For Life umbrella. Most of them would founder through an inability to find suitable housing (local people were often vociferous in their objections to planning permission) or the unwillingness of members of local churches to commit to the projects as wholeheartedly as those of Leeds Reformed Baptist Church had done. There were two exceptions. Light For Life, a rehousing project for homeless young people, providing them with practical and emotional support and advice, was set up in 1990 in Southport, Merseyside, where it continues to operate independently today. In Liverpool, after two years of effort and disappointment, a Drop-in Centre was finally opened in October 1990, under the aegis of Garston Bridge Chapel and its pastor, Bill Bygroves. Run by Jean Brown, who spent several weeks training at Crag House Farm, it was soon hosting a Parents and Tots group and providing advice, support and a weekly low-cost lunch for people living on the streets. Having found its feet with Caring For Life's help, it was successful enough to go independent in September 1991.

In the autumn of 1989, however, Caring For Life was facing a major financial crisis – the first of many. Funds had reached such a low ebb that, one Monday, there was not even enough money available to buy food for the 14 young men in the two homes. 'Aunty Lily', Peter's mother, who did the day-to-day accounts, literally wept when she made this discovery but, within hours, her prayers were miraculously answered. Two local churches had held their harvest festivals the day before and sent their offerings as a gift. Several others followed suit, providing enough fruit, vegetables, bread, tinned food and groceries to keep both homes supplied for a fortnight. This hand-to-mouth existence also affected the ability to employ staff and, without the help of volunteers, it would have been impossible to keep the two homes going. Acute staff-shortages and an ever increasing workload meant that all non-essential tasks had to be temporarily abandoned, including producing a monthly news bulletin for supporters.

There were other difficulties to be overcome. Neighbours living near Carey House were not happy about having such a home in their midst. A meeting was held to attempt to alleviate the situation and strong feelings were expressed but, once the initial antagonism died down, several people expressed an interest in the work of Caring For Life and some even offered to befriend the young men.

Tindall House was experiencing even more serious problems. As the scheduled date for demolition of the estate approached, it had become ever more vulnerable to the depredations of criminal elements. Over the course of the year Tindall House was broken into nine times and a considerable amount of wanton damage was caused. Worse still, the personal possessions of the young men – even items of little value such as their alarm clocks – were stolen. Repeated thefts of this kind undermined all that the staff had been trying to teach the young men in their care, but there was no money available to make the house more secure. The young men themselves were also at considerable risk of being drawn back into offending or addiction because of the presence of criminal gangs, pimps and drug dealers on the estate. Inadvertently Caring For Life added to these problems by agreeing to house two young girls who had been referred to it as a last resort. This proved to be a mistake. Though they had seemed naïve and were clearly in need of just the type of support that the charity could offer, it turned out that they had both been child prostitutes and their continued presence in a house full of vulnerable young men was too disruptive to be countenanced.

Despite all the other financial pressures, the need to find a replacement for Tindall House was becoming an urgent priority. In the spring of 1990 a property in Headingley was identified which had the potential to accommodate all the current residents in a much more pleasant environment. Unable to raise the sale price of £95,000 from the commercial market to buy the house, Caring For Life turned once again to its Christian supporters, who responded with such generosity that a mortgage was obtained and the purchase was completed in September. Work began immediately on making the essential alterations and improvements necessary before the young men could move in. The new Tindall House formally opened its doors to eight residents in December 1990, just in time for them to celebrate Christmas together in their new home.

By that time, however, the work of Caring For Life had taken an entirely new and unexpected turn.

3

Innocents Abroad

The first shocking pictures of the children locked away in Romanian institutions were broadcast to the world at the beginning of 1990. The Western world had never seen anything like it. Vast dormitories with row upon regimented row of cots, each one containing filthy, skeletal babies lying dull-eyed and covered in sores on urine-soaked and faecal-stained mattresses; some were too sick or apathetic to stir; some constantly rocked backwards and forwards or banged their heads against the cot sides like caged wild animals; others were crudely tied to their cots to prevent them moving at all. Many were dying of hypothermia, tuberculosis or HIV/AIDS, the last caused by the multiple use of infected needles. Without pictures, toys, proper clothing or bedding, and lacking all but the most basic human contact to keep them alive, these were the children of Romania's communist regime.

Nicolae Ceaușescu, leader of the communist party and Romania's president for 21 years, had been determined to increase the country's population, despite the poverty of its people. In 1967 he prohibited abortion and contraception for anyone with fewer than four children, resulting in a soaring birth rate and the abandonment into state care of babies whom their parents could not afford to keep or did not want because they had a disability. By the time Ceaușescu was overthrown and executed in the bloody revolution of December 1989, there were more than 100,000 children in some 600 state institutions in a country the size of Great Britain.[10]

The plight of this 'lost generation'[11] in eastern Europe could not fail to touch the hearts of those working for Caring For Life. In April 1990 Peter Parkinson wrote a letter to all the supporters:

> Since commencing the work of Caring For Life, our motto and aim has become quite simply 'Sharing the Love of Jesus'. In living out this motto with the many needy young people whom we have been asked to help, and who are turning to us for counsel, support or friendship, our ministry has, of necessity, expanded far more broadly and rapidly than we had ever anticipated . . . The vision which has encaptured us, of sharing the love of Jesus, demands that we seize new opportunities for ministry as God in His Sovereign grace opens new doors!

Romania was just one of those doors, presenting a radically new and challenging area of Christian ministry. The need was obvious, just as it had been in Leeds: the abandoned

---

10 William Horsley, 'Romania's bloody revolution', BBC News, 22 December 1999: www.news.bbc.co.uk; Kate McGeown, 'What happened to Romania's orphans?', BBC News, 7 August 2005: www.newsvote.bbc.co.uk.

11 Pierre Poupard, head of Unicef in Romania, quoted in www.news vote.bbc.co.uk, p. 1.

children needed homes, medical supplies, food, clothing, bedding, fuel and dedicated, loving care. The enormity of this task was even more daunting than that facing Caring For Life in 1987, but now, at least, the charity had had three years of relevant experience to equip it to take up the challenge. The international project was launched.

The first practical response to the crisis was to plough up enough land at Crag House Farm to supply fresh vegetables to feed 400 people; the hope was that by August it would be possible to send weekly deliveries of fresh and tinned produce to Romania. Appeals were made for volunteers to co-ordinate support groups in collecting non-perishable food, clothing and equipment to send to Romania, and for doctors, nurses, physiotherapists, joiners, electricians, builders, plasterers and plumbers who would be prepared to give a minimum of two weeks' service in eastern Europe. Aware that the new venture would divert the time and energy of some of the staff away from the charity's work in Leeds, it was decided to launch a new scheme that was billed as 'a unique opportunity for Christian voluntary service'. The idea was to invite young Christians over the age of 21 to spend 12 months doing residential, day-care and manual work in the Caring For Life homes and at Crag House Farm. All the participants would take part in a Youth Leadership Training Course and receive in-service training; they would be provided with free board and lodging and be paid a nominal weekly allowance. The purpose of the scheme – christened the TFJ or Time For Jesus project – was to provide voluntary staff to ease the pastoral burden and workload of existing staff and thereby enable the charity to expand its ministry more quickly than its finances would otherwise allow. A role for the TFJs was also envisaged in Romania, so a current passport and driving licence were also requested.

In May 1990, Peter and Esther led a group of volunteers on a fact-finding trip to Transylvania, the western region of Romania, where the revolution had begun in the cities of Timisoara and Arad.[12] It had been agreed that Caring For Life should explore every means possible to try to 'share the love of Jesus' with some of the desperately needy children whose plight had been highlighted in the Western world by media coverage. The trustees were anxious to take advice from local people first and to see the conditions for themselves. They took with them three lorry-loads of food and clothing to distribute where the need was greatest, but nothing had prepared them for the scale and depth of the poverty they encountered. Worse still were the sights that greeted them in the state orphanages they were allowed to visit.[13] Even the best one, in Timisoara, had neither the money nor the staff to provide anything more than rudimentary individual care. Fifty babies were kept in one dormitory and all the toddlers who were capable of walking had to endure long periods of

---

12 Demonstrations in Timisoara against the harassment of a dissident Protestant Hungarian minister had swiftly built up into a mass protest, fuelled by anger at food shortages. The army, acting under Ceauşescu's personal orders, fired on the crowds and killed large numbers, including women and children who were trying to take refuge in the church. Arad was the second city to take up the revolution; it had also played an important role in the nineteenth-century fight for Hungarian independence from the Habsburg empire.

13 They were refused entry to some institutions.

communal potty-sitting. As a video made at the time demonstrates, two 'problem' infants, who were unable to speak, were pinned to the wall in their highchairs by a table and left to fend for themselves without any form of occupation or stimulation. That this was not a one-off situation was demonstrated by the fact that the table had two child-sized semi-circles cut out of the side that was pushed to the wall. Nevertheless, the staff showed some affection for their charges and at least two of them, a doctor and a speech therapist, were Christians. In conversation with them and their friends, the Caring For Life team discovered, most unusually for Romania, that their ideas and aims were almost identical. Their shared vision was to transfer the children out of the vast impersonal institutions into smaller units, each headed by a housemother who would care for a 'family' group of from eight to twelve children, including siblings who had previously been separated under the Ceauşescu regime. Although Caring For Life staff would initially run the homes, it was the intention that they would work themselves out of a job within five years by training up local people to take their place.

This initial trip to Romania forged useful links with both individuals and churches in the cities of Arad and Timisoara which persuaded the Caring For Life team that further involvement in Romania would be viable. (Short-term relief in the shape of lorries taking monthly deliveries of food, clothing and medical supplies to needy individuals, families and villages was already established and on-going.) The decision was taken to appoint an international director, who was recommended to the charity by the editor of a

Christian magazine because he had worked for many years in Romania before the revolution and was already co-ordinating and managing a number of relief projects in the country. The formalities were completed by December 1990, and Caring For Life, or Grija Pentru Viata as it was known in Romanian, became the first trust to be registered in Romania for 47 years and the first Christian trust ever to be registered there.

Aware of the antagonism that some aid organizations had caused by their lack of sensitivity to Romanian culture and of the dangers of Westerners venturing into a country that was already infamous for its corruption, violence and instability, Caring For Life consulted the British Embassy and drew up a code of conduct to which all staff and volunteers were required to subscribe. Much of this was simple good manners, for example, not taking photographs or giving presents to children without asking permission first, but there was also useful practical guidance. Despite their poverty, Romanians were generous in offering hospitality to Western visitors: this should be accepted because to refuse would cause offence, but visitors should never leave without discreetly giving their hosts a carrier bag of food which would more than replace that which had been given.

Caring For Life had entered Romania with the object of setting up a small family home that would be a model for other children's homes. Unfortunately, their new-found Romanian contacts had other ideas and entered into negotiations with local government officials for a large state orphanage in Arad. This had housed 200 babies and was in need of complete refurbishment, so the prefecture of the city was anxious to put it into the hands of a Western charity that would be able to renovate it totally and fund it for the future. The building was clearly too large for what Caring For Life really wanted to do but, under pressure to make a decision, it agreed that it would be possible to divide it into four small homes, each one to be individually run as a family unit. Caring For Life accepted the use of the building in September 1990 and, with an optimism that proved entirely misplaced, declared that it would open the new home on 1 November.

Though volunteers were ready, willing and able to begin work immediately, there were formidable problems to be overcome, not least because of the chaotic state of local government in Romania after the revolution. Transitional arrangements put in place by the new National Salvation Front running the country meant that local mayors and county governors were appointed by central government pending local elections that were then repeatedly postponed. Many of those appointed were communist officials of the former regime who had no interest in promoting the fundamental reforms promised at national level. Corruption was rife, even among those who had suffered most under the old regime and had most to gain from a reformed state; people who had displayed great moral fibre under persecution and been heroes during the time of adversity were now corrupted by the desire for money and power. As one of Caring For Life's Romanian friends observed, 'What Ceauşescu failed to do in 49 years, the American dollar has done in six months.' And, as Caring For Life was to discover to its cost, post-revolution, not only was corruption endemic, but also no one was sure which officials or departments wielded the ultimate power of decision-making.

Clearance to move into the property was eventually obtained after much delay and difficulty, only for the gruesome discovery that many terminally ill children had been left there, whose fate had not yet been decided by the government. Back in England, the charity ruefully made plans to look after them, only to find that, without their knowledge, the children had been removed and no one knew where they had gone. The property had been severely damaged by flooding caused when the previous occupants removed a sink without turning off the water supply, and planning permission had to be obtained to make the necessary structural changes. Remedial work on the building did not begin until April 1991 when teams of volunteers from the UK started to re-wire and re-plumb the main building ready for its conversion into four units. Baths, sinks and toilets were all donated by well-wishers, as was most of the electrical equipment. This was not always achieved without effort. On 25 April, despite several weeks spent soliciting donations from companies and a lorry booked to carry electrical equipment to Arad two days later, there was nothing to put in it and it seemed that the trip would have to be cancelled. At 3.30 p.m. that day, one of the TFJs contacted an electrical distributor called, ironically, Panic Engineering, which had only two employees. They decided to help and rang round all their contacts to such good effect that £14,000 worth of equipment was donated within 24 hours, allowing a full lorry-load to set off as planned.

With applications pouring in for places at the new home, now named Casa Noastra, 'Our Home', Caring For Life decided not to wait for the renovation work to be completed but to open a second home in Paulis, a village a few miles east of Arad. This was exactly the sort of place the charity had wanted from the first: a large, eight-bedroomed property which was purchased entirely with money donated by individual supporters of the charity. It too needed renovation, including the installation of electricity and plumbing, but not on the same scale as Casa Noastra. The first two children were taken into Casa Bucuriei, 'Home of Joy', in May 1991. Paul, aged three, and his two-year-old sister Adina had been abandoned by their mother; their grandmother had taken them in but she was unable to continue looking after them, especially as Adina was physically disabled. She had spent the first year of her life in hospital and, as a result of being strapped down in her cot and numerous injections, the muscles in her legs had failed to develop properly and she was unable to bend her knees. Paul and Adina were joined almost immediately by three children whose father had abandoned them and whose mother was terminally ill with cancer; the eldest child, eleven-year-old Neli, had nursed her mother to the end in a two-roomed hovel, supported only by daily visits from the staff of Caring For Life. The charity had hoped to be able to provide a home also for the two mentally disturbed children whose plight in the orphanage at Timisoara had been so distressing. Extensive efforts were made to find them; it was said that they had been given up for international adoption and they were traced as far as Denmark, but there the trail went cold. Their ultimate fate could only be guessed at and feared.

In order to ensure that the highest standards of childcare were practised in the new homes, the key Romanian employees were brought to England to attend training courses at Crag House Farm. All the care staff were required to undertake basic courses in nutrition, food hygiene and first aid: these were essential in a country where typhoid was endemic, the public water supply was often turned off during the day, and soap and disinfectant were unaffordable luxuries for the majority of the population. The assistant housemothers were also taught more advanced courses, equipping them to deal with children who had been physically, sexually or emotionally abused, had specific behavioural difficulties or had serious health problems such as Hepatitis B and HIV/AIDS. The physical, emotional, psychological, educational and spiritual needs of the children were emphasized, as were their rights to dignity, equality, respect and affection, regardless of their age, background or perceived disability. Visits to various establishments in Leeds, including a day nursery, a children's home and a home for the elderly, were also arranged to demonstrate good practice being put into effect. Before the Romanians returned home, David Hinchliffe, the MP for Wakefield, hosted a reception in the House of Commons to celebrate the work of Caring For Life. It was attended by both British and Romanian staff, the Romanian Ambassador, the British Minister for Overseas Development and many others who had given the charity advice or help in setting up the Romanian project.

The celebrations were premature. Only two months later Peter Parkinson had to go to Arad himself to sort out problems between some of the Romanian staff and, two months further down the line, he had to return again. This time there were also serious concerns that British support for the work in Romania was haemorrhaging away because the slow progress at Casa Noastra, in particular, meant that children had still not been received into its care. In fact, the whole future of this part of the project was in doubt. The Arad District Health Department had taken Caring For Life to court to challenge its right to use the building, declaring that it owned the former orphanage, that the prefecture had exceeded its authority in giving Caring For Life its use in the first place, and that the charity had no proper title to the property. The Health Department won a judgement in its favour, necessitating an appeal to the Supreme Court. The prefecture, which had always been supportive of the charity's work, joined the appeal, and testimonials to the good work it had already done were presented by David Hinchliffe and the British Ambassador in Romania. Nevertheless, the court case would drag on for a year until it was finally decided in Caring For Life's favour in May 1992.

There had also been a serious falling out among some of the key Romanian associates in Arad which threatened to undermine the charity's ability to carry out its work. This was largely due to their inability to work within the management structures that Caring For Life required, but the problems were exacerbated by the fact that the British and Romanian staff were trying to operate at a distance of over 1,500 miles from each other and in the difficult conditions of post-revolutionary Romania. The best-laid plans often went awry simply because vital building materials or items of equipment did not arrive at the time and date expected, or because of a lack of skilled labour among the Romanian workmen. A simple case in point was that tremendous efforts had been made to install a central heating system in both homes before the onset of winter, when temperatures could fall as low as minus 30 degrees. This was finally achieved by the beginning of December 1991, but then the government announced a new tax which effectively meant that no transport was available to bring fuel oil from Austria into Romania. With none available in Romania and only two days' supply for the homes left, Peter Parkinson was driven to appeal for help to the MEP for Leeds, Michael McGowan. With his aid, and that of the Romanian Embassy, a delivery of 28,000 litres was made just in time.

In order to address some of these problems, Caring For Life embarked on a radical overhaul of its Romanian organization in January 1992. A new management structure was drawn up which made more explicit the division between the pastoral and business categories of its work and defined the roles and responsibilities of each member of staff. All senior personnel would be twinned with British staff who, in the case of the housemothers in charge, would in future actually be based in Casa Noastra and Casa Bucuriei and would commit to attending Romanian language lessons.

Irene West, a member of Leeds Reformed Baptist Church who was a trained special needs teacher, went out to Casa

Bucuriei in January 1992. She had spent a month working as a volunteer for Caring For Life in Romania the previous summer and had been 'smitten' by both the place and the children:

> The place was full of contrasts and, in some ways, amazingly basic. I remember the village houses that were literally made of straw and mud, with mud floors – and yet despite houses sharing a well in the street some of them had satellite television (which I didn't have at home at the time). As Westerners we were considered to have endless resources – *Dallas* was the most watched programme and many Romanians thought that we all lived like the people on the show. We tried to provide for the staff and their families, as it would be hard seeing things your own children didn't have being given to the children of Casa Bucuriei.

Irene arrived at a time when inflation was running at an appallingly high rate and, as a consequence, actual poverty was increasing, with terrible consequences. In the Director's office in the main hospital of Arad, a chart proudly displayed the fact that infant mortality in the area had been slashed – to just 24%. (In the UK the comparable figure was 0.8%.) The school classroom in Paulis had one light bulb, which was moved around the six light fittings to wherever it was most needed. The price of a bus ticket had increased tenfold in the two years since the revolution and there were long queues for basic supplies. Irene remembers being '80-something' in a queue for eggs, but 'at least there were some available that week' and there was sometimes a 24-hour wait for petrol. (Irene discovered that the best time to go to queue for petrol was when *Dallas* was on the television!) Obtaining medical care for the children was just as difficult: even if medicines and equipment were available, which they often were not, the system relied on taking 'gifts' for the doctors. Everyday life was an energy-sapping battle and it was all too easy for the ordinary working Romanians to become discouraged and pessimistic about their future.

When Irene arrived there were already five (soon to rise to nine, then twelve) children in Casa Bucuriei; they came from five sibling groups and were between 21 months and 14 years of age:

> The children just stole your heart. Most of them were skinny when they came to us and most of them had to be shown how to shower, flush toilets, etc. The hardest bit was convincing them that we, and God, would love them no matter what.

For the Romanian staff, as much as for the children, it was a learning process. They had to be taught that, while the children's behaviour was not always lovable, the children themselves as individuals were still to be loved unconditionally, just as God loves us. It was an unusual message, even among Romanian Christians, where the tradition was, and in some places still remains, that 'God will not love you if you are bad'. Visitors to Casa Bucuriei even in these early days noted that it was a noisy and happy home where the children felt free to shout, sing and play; but they were also moved by their tender and affectionate response to new children coming into the home and by their natural and spontaneously expressed piety. There was a particularly warm welcome for three of the children who returned to the home in April 1993 after spending several months in England for medical treatment that was unobtainable in Romania. Specialists had offered to treat them free of charge and a local fund in Leeds raised enough money to pay their travel costs, something that Caring For Life could not itself afford to do. One of the children was Adina, who was able to bend her knees for the first time when the plaster casts were removed three weeks after her operation, and was soon a menace to anyone in the vicinity as she took great delight in tearing around on a tricycle.

While Casa Bucuriei flourished, the future of Casa Noastra remained uncertain. The court case still languished unresolved though all the advice from both sides appeared to be that Caring For Life would be allowed to continue using the property, even if the decision went against it. A bad winter had demonstrated that it would be essential to re-roof the building, an additional expense that had not been included in the budget. That budget was already under severe pressure. Expenditure in Romania in the 12 months to January 1992 alone had been almost £260,000, half of which was represented by the value of donated goods, and the books only just balanced. Staffing costs were running at £3,500 a month and more would be needed when Casa Noastra opened, yet less money was coming in. This was not just a phenomenon felt by Caring For Life. The plight of Romania had been overtaken in the public mind by equally distressing crises in Albania, Sudan and Bosnia, and compassion fatigue had set in among donors and supporters.

Despite generous gifts from other charities and individuals, and another working trip by volunteer electricians and plumbers, in the end money had to be borrowed to complete the conversion work. This proceeded at snail's pace, not least because unemployment levels in the country were so high that the charity felt morally obligated to employ Romanian labour as far as possible. In an effort to cut costs, it was decided to dispense with the idea of creating a fourth family unit and to open a day-care centre in its place. Even so, it was not until just before Christmas 1992 – more than two years after the property had been given to Caring For Life – that the first family unit at Casa Noastra finally opened as a home for eight children, ranging from 2 months to 14 years of age.

The opening of Casa Noastra as a properly functioning children's home ought to have allowed Caring For Life's work in Romania to forge ahead but, instead, it merely brought all the existing difficulties into focus and compounded them. Finances were increasingly an issue. The Romanians believed that Caring For Life had a bottomless purse and expected that all their requests for money would be paid immediately and without question. As a charity reliant on donations, Caring For Life had always been acutely aware of its responsibility to account for every penny of expenditure and to ensure that the money was spent in the most efficient and effective way possible. Staff in England therefore demanded receipts, queried discrepancies in exchange rates (the Romanians could not understand why Caring For Life refused to countenance exchanging money at the more favourable rates available on the black market), and refused to pay bills for unsubstantiated costs. The Romanians naturally found this offensive and reacted angrily, believing that it cast doubt on their honesty. Nevertheless, though it was clear that their financial administration was also at fault, there were increasing grounds for genuine suspicion of corrupt practices. Some 16,000 of the 28,000 litres of fuel oil sent in December 1991 and intended for Casa Noastra had disappeared without trace. Valuable tools, building materials, food and clothing sent to the home had also gone missing to a degree that implied more than simple negligence. Money known to have been given directly to the charity's Romanian associates by American visitors to the homes never appeared in Caring For Life's bank, or in accounts in Romania, or in the monthly financial accounts sent to Leeds.

The breakdown in trust between the British and Romanians was exacerbated by disagreement over how Casa Noastra should be run. The fundamental principles had always been clear and were consistently reiterated in training. Caring For Life homes should be places where children grew up as brothers and sisters in an environment as close as possible to that of a normal family home; any tendency towards institutionalization should be avoided; staff should maintain as natural a relationship with the children as possible, with the senior housemother in each home fulfilling the mother-figure role and offering both security and authority; each child should be seen as a God-created human being and, as such, should be treated with dignity and respect and protected from any form of mental, physical, emotional, verbal, sexual or social abuse or discrimination, in pursuit of which the privacy of each child and home must be respected at all times; and, finally, since the homes were to be Christian homes, it was essential that all the staff be sincere and committed Christians of high moral calibre and integrity.

Though this was close to being achieved at Casa Bucuriei, even there the principle that the senior housemother was the most important member of the staff in a residential context had been undermined by Romanian associates and administrative staff from Arad who claimed (and practised) ultimate authority. The privacy of the home and the children was constantly breached by unannounced visits and there were several occasions when American guests, in particular, were brought uninvited into the children's bedrooms and, without permission, filmed them there. Once, the children were even required to do several takes to camera of saying grace before breakfast before they were allowed to eat. The situation was worse at Casa Noastra where the Romanian administration was based and an unauthorized relocation of the offices meant that non-residential staff had to walk through the children's playroom to get to their place of work. The homely atmosphere of the three units, which each had their own bathroom and kitchen as well as lounge and bedrooms, was also undermined by a decision to cook all the food centrally and make the housemothers collect it for distribution.

This not only created a more institutionalized atmosphere but also made it more difficult to teach the children the culinary skills they would need for the future. Relations between individual Romanians were also at rock bottom and had an adverse effect on the creation of a loving and homely environment for the children.

Caring For Life had always been aware of the dangers of working in Romania. Its code of conduct had stressed the importance of carrying money and documents securely about the person, of being cautious about accepting invitations from strangers and of never travelling alone at night, stopping in isolated areas or leaving vehicles unattended in public places. Although there had been scary incidents before, the most terrifying occurred in the spring of 1993. A Romanian member of staff was supposed to collect Esther Smith from Casa Noastra and take her to the airport in Hungary for her flight back to England. He did not come, but someone else arrived in his place who, instead of taking her to the airport, drove her over the Hungarian border and then claimed that his car had broken down. He flagged down a Turkish lorry, spoke to the driver, and told her that he had arranged for him to take her to the airport. Esther objected, tried and failed to flag down one of the European aid vehicles driving past, then begged to be allowed to stay with her driver until his car was fixed. He refused, so she was left with no option but to get into the lorry.

It was not until after they had set off that she realized there was a second driver in the cab. The two men tried to engage her in conversation in various languages, but she pretended that she did not understand. They then pulled into a lay-by surrounded by woodland and began a furious argument – unaware that she understood something of what they were saying. Terrified that she would be raped or killed, she began to cry and pray: in her own heart she said goodbye to the Tindall House boys and everyone she loved, apologizing to them for 'letting them down' because she would not be there for them in the future. At that moment, inexplicably, the men angrily turned on her, threw her and her bags out of the lorry, and drove off at high speed. Esther made her way to the edge of the woodland where, to her enormous relief, she could see a group of women working on the fields in the distance. She managed to explain her plight to them and they took her back to their village where they found her a taxi.

Her difficulties were not yet over. Esther did not have any Hungarian currency with her because she had expected to be delivered straight to the airport. When the taxi driver asked her what cash she had, she explained that she only had American dollars. He then took everything she had and delivered her to the airport where, absolutely distraught, she discovered that she was in the wrong place. Fortunately, some military personnel took pity on her and drove her to the correct destination. There she was allowed to ring Caring For Life in England and Peter was able to pay by credit card for another flight for her via Paris. Peter himself drove to London to pick her up. It was a traumatic experience that underscored the very real physical danger of working in Romania. And since there was neither explanation nor apology from

anyone in Arad, the incident further soured relations between Romania and Leeds.

A last-ditch attempt was made to resolve the problems by
sending out Graham Sharkey, a trusted member of Leeds Reformed Baptist Church who was a pharmacist with business
experience, spoke Romanian and had spent many months
working for Caring For Life in Romania. Even though he
had been appointed executive director of the international
project, he was refused access to bank statements, discovered
that Romanian directors had instructed that no records of
money spent or goods received were to be kept, and was for-
cibly ejected from Casa Noastra. Both he and Irene, who was
still persevering in her post at Casa Bucuriei, were told that
they should leave Romania immediately and have no further
contact with the homes or the organization.

Since it was now clear that the relationship had broken
down completely, Caring For Life felt that it had no other
recourse than temporarily to suspend financial and material
support to Romania. Subsequent legal advice from Foreign
Office appointed lawyers revealed that, because both homes
were registered in Romania, Caring For Life had no existing legal right to control the use of the properties, nor to
insist on adherence to standards of childcare acceptable to
itself and its supporters. It was an untenable position from
which there were only three viable ways forward. The first
and preferred option was to remove the Romanian management committee and run the two homes directly with British
personnel, in which case Caring For Life would continue to
accept complete financial responsibility. The second was for

Caring For Life to have total control of, and financial responsibility for, Casa Bucuriei but to relinquish management of Casa Noastra to the Romanian administration of the charity, continuing to provide advice and training but only a minimum of financial assistance. The third and least favoured option was for Caring For Life to withdraw from the country completely, leaving their Romanian associates and staff to run both homes under a different name.

No formal response was received to this assessment of the situation, but the leading Romanian associate was adamant in correspondence with intermediaries that his country's law did not permit a Romanian trust to be run by foreign 'dictatorship' – a view that was confirmed by Caring For Life's own lawyers in Budapest. When the latter also advised that British personnel might be at risk by remaining in Romania in such highly charged circumstances, the decision had to be taken to order them home for their own safety. On 10 June 1993, Caring For Life formally withdrew from Romania.

The failure of the Romanian project was a source of bitter disappointment and much soul-searching for all involved. There were some straws of comfort. Two children's homes had been established and would continue to run successfully, if not up to the high pastoral standards demanded by Caring For Life. Many Romanians, in addition to the children, had benefited from the aid supplied. And a lasting legacy had been left in the form of training Romanian staff on how to run model small-group children's homes.

The painful truth that had to be faced, however, was that the charity had promised to 'care for life' for the children and had reneged on that promise. Many supporters who had given generously and even sacrificially of their time and money felt betrayed by what they saw as an 'abandonment' of the children to an uncertain future. Though some churches and individuals took the view that their support had been given to the children, not to the charity, which had only been the means and not the end, others were not convinced and severed relations with Caring For Life itself. The whole experience had proved extremely costly, not just financially, but also in terms of goodwill towards Caring For Life and in diverting staff time and energy from what they now realized should have been their core work in Leeds. Important lessons had been learned. Caring For Life had overreached itself. One door had been closed, but others remained open.

4

Locks and Keys

Though the urgency of the need in Romania had made working in that country a priority, Caring For Life's burden at home had not diminished. Rather, as its reputation spread more widely among agencies dealing with the homeless, the number of referrals it received had risen to two or three every single day. This was part of a disturbing national trend. Homelessness was increasing and its nature was changing. The introduction of the Care in the Community programme in 1991 opened the floodgates as a large number of residential psychiatric hospitals were forced to close. Many of those released should never have been in such institutions at all but had been committed decades earlier for perceived moral failings, such as having a baby outside marriage, which had then been regarded as evidence of mental incapacity. Nevertheless, even those who did not have serious psychiatric problems when they entered the hospital had been left incapable of independent living through years of institutionalization. Care in the Community was introduced too quickly and without adequate provision of money or supportive services for these desperately vulnerable people, who rapidly slipped into homelessness. Caring For Life saw its rate of referrals quadruple as a result and, as the vast majority had some form of mental illness, it had to change the way it looked after them, most especially by ensuring that it employed only appropriately trained staff.

The rising rates of homelessness in Leeds were no different from those in any other major city in the country. The St Anne's Centre, the largest centre serving the homeless in Leeds, had seen 1,500 people in 1991, a 22% increase on the previous year. The waiting list for local authority housing in 1992 stood at just over 24,000 households, including 1,248 households (households, it should be emphasized, not individuals) that were either already homeless or about to become homeless.[14]

What was perhaps even more worrying about this trend was that so many of the new homeless were extremely young. Nightstop, the charity founded in Leeds in 1987, which offered safe emergency accommodation for 16- to 25-year-olds in the homes of approved volunteers, reported that 70% of their referrals in the spring of 1992 were aged 16. Though the Children Act of 1989 had required local authorities to house children under 18, they had not been given the resources to do so and appropriate housing was in very short supply. Among the latest referrals to Caring For Life at this time were a 16-year-old schoolboy thrown out of his family home that morning and a 15-year-old girl, due to have a baby in seven weeks' time, who had drifted in and out of homelessness for

---

14 *Yorkshire Evening Post*, 23 November 1992.

over a year. All that the local authority had been able to offer the boy was a place in a large night shelter mainly used by older vagrants; the only option available for the girl was a large mother and baby home – so she promptly chose to disappear again.

These referrals came at a particularly difficult time for Caring For Life. The pot for charitable giving was finite and many people had diverted their donations to Romania. Although the Romanian side of its operation was well funded at this time, the charity had been struggling financially in England since November 1990. At a crisis meeting in February 1991, the trustees discovered to their horror that they owed debts of £120,000 and there were no funds to pay any of their creditors. Their accountant and financial advisers urged them to cut their losses and close down their English operation, but this they could not contemplate. What would happen to all the young people who depended on them for care for life?

Peter took personal control of the situation. He got in touch with all the creditors and explained the position to each of them quite candidly: he could not even offer them ten pence in the pound if they insisted on immediate settlement of their debt, but if they were prepared to wait, then he promised them that they would be repaid in full by the end of the year. He had no idea how he would fulfil that promise, but he passionately believed that God had blessed Caring For Life's work, that he had performed miracles in the past that had enabled it to survive, and that he would surely do so again, to enable the charity to continue to share the love of Jesus with many more people in the future.

This was the start of the most difficult and distressing period in Caring For Life's history. As an immediate measure, half the staff had to be made redundant, but four of them, Esther Smith, Debbie Habibzadeh and Jonathan and Tim Parkinson, volunteered to continue working without pay. This would enable the homes and the day-care schemes at the farm to remain open and the counselling work to continue. A new accountant, Rachel Rothwell, was appointed and she too generously agreed that she would work without pay for a year. Money was now in such short supply that Esther and the Parkinsons were literally having to live off the land, eating their own produce and supplementing it by shooting rabbits and pigeons in the fields, and pheasants at Christmas time.

In the summer, however, a supporter came to their rescue. He worked for, and was a personal friend of, the owner of a company called No Ordinary Hotels, which had just completed the restoration of the magnificent Lumley Castle in County Durham and opened it as a hotel. Now it was about to embark on another ambitious project, the conversion and refurbishment of Coombe Abbey in Warwickshire and, in order to make the development look more authentic, it needed decorative plasterwork based on historic examples. Caring For Life was given the opportunity to provide plaster busts, statues and cornices. No one at the charity had any previous experience in this type of work, but it was an opportunity that could not be missed. The company sent some moulds, casts and materials, and provided an expert to show them how it was done. Tim and Debbie were given the task of making the casts, assisted principally by Gary from Tindall House, then

Debbie would finish them off, decorating them so that they looked authentic. The first set of sample busts they produced were of such good quality that the company had no hesitation in awarding them the contract for all the work, and so for the next four months they literally worked night and day producing thousands of casts, delivering them to Coventry and then driving back again to begin work on the next batch. They worked frantically to complete and install productions for Christmas, finally arriving back from Coombe Abbey at six o'clock on Christmas Eve morning. By the time the contract had been completed, in the summer of 1992, they had earned £80,000 and had contributed massively to saving Caring For Life. Enough money was scraped together to fulfil Peter's promise to pay back all their creditors, except one feed manufacturer who was willing to wait a little longer for his payment. The charity would live to fight another day.

Shortly afterwards, Carey House in Yeadon had to be returned to its owner. Though none of its residents was forced to leave, Caring For Life temporarily had to stop accepting any residential referrals until there were enough places at the new Tindall House to accommodate all those who remained. With its own ability to offer accommodation reduced, the only way to help the increasing number of young people being referred was to find them homes in the community. This was impossible without funding for the necessary staff but, by God's grace, the very same month that Carey House closed, Caring For Life received its first grant from the Department of the Environment. This allowed a resettlement team to be established whose remit was to establish a relationship with homeless young people who were referred to them, assess their immediate needs, then provide them with practical help in the form of finding and furnishing accommodation and helping them to move in. Assistance would be given in sorting out benefits, organizing budgets and training in life-skills. Individual counselling would also be available and the young people would be encouraged to look for work, go to college, or join the day-care scheme at the farm. They would be visited in their own homes on a daily, twice-weekly or weekly basis – depending on their level of need – for as long as they wanted, but the team would always be on call whenever something went wrong.

With local authority housing stock already vastly over-subscribed, and housing associations also under immense pressure, the only option available was to look to private landlords to fill the need. Private landlords, however, were reluctant to accept young people with drug, alcohol or mental health problems, having experienced difficulties in the past with vandalizing or neglect of properties and with non-payment of rents caused by frequent delays in the processing of housing benefit applications. Most landlords demanded a bond of a month's rent in advance and references from both bank and employer, creating a Catch 22 situation whereby it was impossible to get a house unless you had a job, but impossible to get a job unless you had a house. Someone who fell into this trap was Mark, a 24-year-old welder, who became homeless when his relationship ended and his girl-friend threw him out of their house. He had nowhere else to go so ended up living for two weeks in a big city hostel for homeless men. 'As soon as I was here, the chance of a job disappeared. They just didn't want to know when they found out where I was living.'[15]

This was the sort of situation where Caring For Life could make all the difference, offering private landlords a partnership whereby they provided the accommodation and the charity provided the support that would create a stable and enduring tenancy. As Diane Deacon explained:

> We believe homelessness is not simply a housing problem. We don't just give them the key and then leave them. A lot of these young people need intensive support: they don't just need a roof over their heads, they need specialist care and attention.
>
> We teach them life-skills such as cooking, washing, ironing and basic DIY to help them live independently.[16]

The resettlement team found Mark a room in a shared house owned by a private landlord but he, and others like him, also enjoyed ongoing support. 'We can help the young person with filling in forms and teach them how to budget,' Graham Murly told the *Yorkshire Evening Post* in an attempt to highlight the problem publicly and recruit more private landlords. 'It's also about building up trust. A lot of homeless young people have suffered a great deal of rejection. What they need is a big injection of self-esteem, dignity and respect.'[17]

---

15 *Yorkshire Evening Post*, 23 November 1992.
16 *Leeds Weekly News*, 23 December 1993, p. 17.
17 *Yorkshire Evening Post*, 23 November 1992.

One unusually articulate young man gave a moving insight into how his life had been transformed by the resettlement team: his words appear unedited:

I am crawling on the floor of my hostel room. I am looking for one tiny speck of brown, hoping for a tablet, wanting to go back to where it's peaceful and calm. My brain wants to go there and my body is crawling on the floor trying to keep up.

Just one more tablet. Such a small space between misery and joy. I pick up bits from the floor, flecks of paint, grit, some tobacco. I want to put the needle into my arm, slide it smoothly into the vein. I love the piercing pain that comes just before the waves flood my heart. I am such a dirty junkie!! Help me!! Caring For Life did!!

People abuse themselves in many ways for many reasons. Most people I know, myself included, abuse drugs to fill the void in their hearts, souls and minds left by the disappearance of hope. Hope of remedying their miserable childhoods, of achieving a happy future, a future filled with things so many people take for granted: a comfortable home, a job, someone to love, and someone who loves them. A life without love and hope is an empty and meaningless life.

When faced with such despair, drug abuse seems the only way out.

Caring For Life showed me that there was an alternative. They began to do this by showing that my life had meaning to them even when it had none to me.

My first contact with Caring For Life was through Danny and Graham – who run the resettlement project at Caring For Life. Upon meeting them they expressed a genuine concern for my welfare. They backed up their words with the action of moving me from the rundown hostel I was staying at to a warm and homely shared house. The four other residents of my new home had all experienced the desolation that I was feeling. This showed me that I was not alone. Caring For Life's interest in me did not stop there.

Danny and Graham continued to visit regularly. They came to ensure that I was content. Content with my house and content with my life. Due to Caring For Life's support and this contentment, my desire for escape began to lessen. In other words, drug abuse was beginning to become a thing of the past.

I now live in a flat that Caring For Life has arranged for me and, thanks to help from others involved with Caring For Life, is filled with furniture and all the other things that make a house or a flat a home.

I am now working full time at the farm with horticulture. This has given me a new respect for my environment. My life now has purpose, my life now has meaning. I have stopped abusing drugs, abusing myself, abusing others. I have begun to see a brighter future, and no longer see such a dim past.

The doors of my heart, soul and mind are again both open to hope and love.

I always had the keys – but Caring For Life helped me find the locks.

As this account makes clear, working at Crag House Farm proved crucial in the steps towards this young man's rehabilitation. Even for those with less serious problems, meaningful employment was, and remains, hugely important. It is all too easy to drift into a life of drug abuse or crime simply through boredom, and for many young people, especially those with learning difficulties, life can be extremely boring because they find it difficult to relate to other people, are nervous of going out alone, do not have the initiative to try new things and lack the ability to read a newspaper or follow the plot of a television programme. For those living on their own, loneliness can also be an acute problem. Many of those being helped by the resettlement team see no other visitors from one week to the next. Even those who have been able to move on from the protected environment of Caring For Life's residential homes often feel the need to return. Saturday nights at Tindall House soon became known as 'visitors' night' when past residents were welcome to call in for tea and chat or just to watch television. Inevitably, though, among young men who found it difficult to relate to other people socially, arguments frequently arose. 'All of our young men are desperate for individual attention for themselves and for their own concerns,' the supervisor wrote in 1993. 'Where there is a group each competes for attention at the expense of the others. I often find that I am drawn into three completely unrelated conversations in a group of four people. No one really has my full attention, so no one is happy.'

The day-care provision at Crag House Farm provided opportunities not just for meaningful work but also for learning to act appropriately in social situations, building friendships, sharing problems and receiving counselling. A typical day at the farm began at 8 a.m. with coffee and conversation – with some more awake than others. After a staff prayer meeting, work began on the morning routines: feeding the horses, cows, goats, dogs and hens, and collecting the eggs (up to 1,000 a day). After a lunch-break and the obligatory football match which, in bad weather, was played inside one of the barns, the afternoon was spent preparing the poly-tunnel for the next crop of plants and vegetables and cleaning and renovating the chicken houses ready for the next flock of hens. 'Most of our young people have never had steady work or known the companionship, fun and satisfaction that can go with it,' one of the staff observed in February 1993. After the final routine of feeding and bedding down the animals had been completed, it was time to go home – but not always for all the staff. 'This evening a young man had to be collected from a psychiatric hospital, having discharged himself, against advice. He had attempted suicide two or three times since Christmas and was planning to try again.'

Sadly, this was by no means an unusual conclusion to the day. It is no coincidence that suicide attempts peak during the Christmas period when the rest of the world appears to be enjoying a happy family gathering, reinforcing feelings of rejection and isolation among those living alone. The fact that he was just one of three people, supported by the resettlement team, who had tried to commit suicide over Christmas prompted the decision to invite as many as possible to the farm for Christmas Day the following year. This became an established feature of the year, with a Christmas lunch provided by staff and volunteers, followed by games, songs and finally a period of quiet conversation, contemplation and prayer.

The horticultural project had expanded greatly in the light of the decision to grow vegetables to send to Romania. (Much of the sorting, packing and storing of donated goods for Romania was also done on site by the young people.) This gave them the satisfaction not only of doing something intrinsically useful and productive, but also of doing it to help others even less fortunate than themselves. As the supervisor of Tindall House noted:

> Listening to conversations in the evening as to who has done the most work during the day reveals the pride these young men take in the work they can do. Hypocrisy and exaggeration apart, such discussions show that each young man knows he has a role and a purpose in life through his work at the farm and that he is worthy of some self-respect.

In addition to the vegetables, the project was also growing bedding plants and shrubs to sell to garden centres, local supermarkets and visitors to the farm. By using plug plants, rather than just growing from seed, they were able to involve those with poor motor skills who could simply pull the plugs out by the leaves, take aim, and then drop them into a pot. The degree of control needed to pot on plug plants of varying sizes and sow seed was useful exercise for muscles, brain and, as everyone concerned swiftly learnt, patience. This type of work could be a lifeline for people with a disability that excluded them from other employment. Other more severely disabled children, including those from a local special school, gained enormous benefit from simply stroking animals on the farm or sitting in a field smelling the hay.

It therefore seemed to be a disaster when strong winds on the night of 23 January 1993 lifted and blew away the plastic coverings of the two poly-tunnels. Fortunately, it was not in the middle of the growing season, but the poly-tunnels were essential for the generation of income for the day-care project. Pleas for assistance in erecting new windbreaks demonstrated the enormous generosity of Caring For Life supporters. British Telecom donated 20 telegraph poles, and Worth Trees of Lincolnshire gave 5,000 saplings, which were planted at vulnerable spots throughout the farm. Just as the final batch of trees was planted out, a donation of a further 2,000 arrived.

The enforced withdrawal from Romania, heartbreaking though it had been, gave renewed impetus and focus to all the projects at Crag House Farm. Over the spring and summer of 1993 a large number of volunteers assisted the young people and staff in planting the trees, pricking out seedlings in the new heated seed-tray beds in the poly-tunnel, and selling bedding plants to local shops and visitors. A comprehensive review of all the projects took place and it was realized that, if the young people were to take a pride in what they were doing, their working conditions needed to be improved. The room where many of them spent part of the day cleaning, grading and boxing eggs for sale was totally re-furbished with new tiles on the floor and walls and new lighting, and the Resource Centre was re-dedicated to the use of the young people by relocating the administrative staff, who had virtually taken it over, into new offices in one of the barns. Dry stone walls and fencing were erected to move stock on to fresh grazing land and the hen houses were also refurbished. A new venture, which continues to thrive today, was the result of a gift from Ted Brearly, a supporter and geneticist, who donated some rare guinea pigs to the farm. Their small size, placid nature and soft fur made them ideal objects of care for those young people intimidated by the larger animals. A successful breeding programme (assisted, occasionally, by the young people accidentally mixing the sexes when cleaning out the cages!) enabled them to be taken round the local shows, where the fact that they regularly won prizes was a matter of great pride to those who looked after them.

All these schemes were made possible by the input of volunteers, including the young people themselves. One of these was Nick Kennard, a 21-year-old with cerebral palsy, who was wheelchair bound and had the use of only one hand. Despite struggling to feed himself and being unable to dress without the help of his mother, Nick spent three months building a 40-metre-long path between the poly-tunnels and the Resource Centre so that people could walk easily between the two. The project had been his own idea. He used secondhand bricks to pave the pathway, and shrubs were planted on each side to make its setting more attractive. Sitting areas were also created (Nick called them his 'lay byes'), from which to admire this new garden area and the path itself. A personal triumph for Nick himself, the path was also a valuable addition to the facilities at the farm, particularly for those who were physically disabled.

It is of the very nature of Caring For Life's work with vulnerable people that for every leap forward there are two steps back. This same summer saw the arrest and imprisonment of two much-loved young men whom the Parkinsons and Esther Smith had known since childhood. They had both lived at Foxcroft Children's Home and at Carey House. Andrew had been, and remains to this day, Jonathan Parkinson's closest friend. Brian was a livewire who was constantly in trouble. On one occasion, Jonathan remembers, when they were all at the church camp in Wales, they were sliding down a hillside on sledges improvised from black plastic bin liners. Brian had insisted on flying down backwards with his leg in the air and, inevitably, disappeared into a large area of bracken. When he eventually returned and was asked why he had gone down backwards, he replied, 'I don't want to see what I am going to crash into.' With hindsight, it was a remark that could equally have applied to his entire life.

Though they had graduated to independent accommodation, Andrew and Brian had remained both needy and easily influenced. Within weeks of first leaving Carey House, Brian had lost all his belongings and, after going without food for two days, rang Caring For Life in tears asking 'Can I come home?' Two weeks after leaving for a second time, to live with his girlfriend, he was remanded into custody. Now, having set fire to a garden shed and a car seat, he and Andrew were both facing a 20-year prison sentence for committing arson. The severity of the sentence seemed so shocking and disproportionate (particularly as on the same day the same judge had released a paedophile on probation) that Peter and Esther decided to fight for an appeal. Brian's prospects were especially bad since this was not his first conviction for arson and he had already served a prison sentence some years earlier. In a desperate attempt to prevent him being sent down again, Esther discovered that it might be possible to secure his release if Caring For Life agreed to become his legal guardian in partnership with Social Services. Though this was an innovative interpretation of the law – guardians were assumed to be individual people, not corporate bodies – the judge who presided over the new hearing proved sympathetic. He released Brian into Caring For Life's care under a guardianship order, and Andrew was released on probation. It had been a harrowing time for all concerned, but faith had sustained them. As Andrew wrote to Peter a few days before going to court: 'No matter what happens with this judge on Friday, when I die I will be judged by a righteous Judge who will be merciful and fair.' His gratitude when he learnt that he would not be going to prison for 20 years was equally profound. 'God has been extremely good and gracious, I now appreciate life more than I ever did before and am willing to let God lead me down those paths he chooses, because I now trust him with my life, the life he gave me.'

Andrew and Brian had been offered a new start but for Brian's girlfriend there was no such opportunity. Mary was 29 when she was referred to Caring For Life. Her antisocial and violent behaviour had led to her being rejected by every other agency but, in the few short months that she had been under its wing, she had been re-housed and begun to have more self-esteem; she started to dress better, to smile, joke, and even to apologize for her behaviour. Since Christmas Day she had attended almost every Sunday service at Leeds Reformed Baptist Church, as well as some midweek meetings, and had become a keen member of the Young People's Fellowship. She had even embarked on a self-imposed task of copying out the entire New Testament by hand and had applied for baptism.

As she began to trust people at Caring For Life, she gradually shared some of her tragic story with them. Though its broad outlines can be verified independently, including some of the salient points, not all the detail can be substantiated. Nevertheless, the following is her story as she told it.

Mary had never come to terms with being abandoned by her mother. She had grown up on a 'problem' estate in Leeds and, as a result of sexual abuse, had her first child at the age of 14. To keep her pregnancy a secret, she ran away from home and joined a group of travellers at the other end of the country. When she decided to return home, she left the baby in their care. On disclosing to the authorities that she had been sexually abused for years, she was removed to a children's home in another city. Though this was done for her own protection, it also separated her from everyone she knew. Mary's insecurity and anger made her increasingly violent and uncontrollable – she thought nothing of smashing her fist through a car window if someone upset her – so she was moved from one home to another. When she finally left care, she drifted from place to place: hostels for women, bedsits or squats with friends, returning home occasionally to her family. She had three further children, but these were all removed from her and taken into care as they were deemed to be severely at risk. A fifth child, which she had hoped to be allowed to keep, was born prematurely and only lived for a couple of days. The same year she learned that her first child, now 14, had been found brutally murdered.

Constantly hounded by her past and deeply insecure, Mary was desperate for attention. Careless of her safety and willing to try any drug or experience to blot out her unhappiness and pain, she frequently took overdoses or slashed her wrists. Only two days after she had been warned that there would come a day when her suicide attempt might succeed, she took her own life, whether accidentally or deliberately no one would ever know.

Mary's unexpected death was a great shock to everyone who had known her, including many of her childhood friends who were now being looked after by Caring For Life. It was particularly devastating for her boyfriend Brian, coming only four months after his release from prison. The grief of the staff was compounded by a sense of failure, guilt and self-reproach. Peter's words summed up their feelings. 'I am all too conscious that I as a minister of the gospel have done far too little; that we at Caring For Life have done far too little; that all of us as Christians have done far too little; yet who can be equal to the task before us?'

Only four months later, there would be another challenge to what Peter called the 'woefully inadequate' nature of Caring For Life's ministry. Alan was friendly and polite, a gentle giant of a man, whose strong, capable and outwardly untroubled appearance belied his emotional insecurities and inadequacies. That was when he was sober and clean. At the age of 13 he had begun to sniff glue, the start of the slippery slope to chronic solvent, drug and alcohol abuse that left him uncontrollable. As a result, he had been ejected from, and rejected by, most hostels in Leeds. By the time the probation service referred him to Caring For Life he was described as 'the most difficult young man we are dealing with'. Like Mary, he had begun to respond to the love and support he was offered. In January he had accompanied the Tindall House residents on their annual trip to Center Parcs and, over the next couple of months, had settled well into the farm environment, building relationships with all the staff and the young people too. Although he had also attended church and appeared anxious to sort himself out and lead a normal life, he still stumbled at every hurdle. He was unable to cope with being on his own for any length of time and needed the constant companionship of the staff to support him; as soon as he mixed with people of similar disposition to himself his resistance to drug and solvent abuse simply collapsed and he became suicidal. 'It's my life,' he told the staff. 'I didn't ask to be born and I don't want to live. If I want to take my life I will. If I want to take my life with drugs I will.' Although Alan had made many attempts on his life in a misguided appeal for love and attention, he eventually died of natural causes. The accumulation of chemicals in his body after years of solvent abuse proved too much for him and his heart failed. He was just 22.

Alan's death was yet another reminder of the desperate plight of vast numbers of homeless, vulnerable and lonely young people. His need had been urgent and the time to help him had been so short. Once again, Peter put the questions that had to be asked. 'What more should we have done? What more could we have done? In what ways did we fail Alan? Could we have done more? Why didn't we do more?'

5

Drops in the Ocean

One way to do more was to expand the day-care projects at Crag House Farm. The old Dutch barn at the farm had been declared unsafe. Characteristically, instead of this being a problem, it was seen as an opportunity: it could be demolished and a new barn and workshops built on the site. Though this was undoubtedly a good idea, making it happen would be difficult as the cost was prohibitive. (A recent appeal to supporters to fund an extra member of staff as a workshop training supervisor had struggled to raise enough money to pay his salary for six months.) The ingenious solution was to appeal to *Action Time*, a Yorkshire Television programme broadcast every month throughout the Yorkshire and Tyne Tees region. Much like its more famous BBC model *Challenge Anneka*, the aim of the programme was to help voluntary organizations with building projects by drawing on the sponsorship and skills of companies and volunteers.

The project attracted an enormous response. More than 80 businesses and numerous individuals offered their help, including Severfield-Reeve, a steel manufacturer based in Thirsk in North Yorkshire, which donated 8 tonnes of steel and provided the workmen to build the new training centre. A team of bricklayers from Birmingham, an electrician from Sunderland and two of the local Leeds Rugby League stars were among the many volunteers who joined the staff and young people in the building work. The brand-new workshop was officially opened by Yorkshire Television presenters on 4 September 1995 to a great fanfare in the local media.[18]

There was still much internal work to be done, so this became the first and most urgent task of the new Workshop Training Supervisor, Rob Newby (who had first worked for Caring For Life as a volunteer plumber refurbishing the children's homes in Romania), and his team of young people. By Christmas they had installed drains, a disabled toilet and a central heating system and, under Jonathan Parkinson's supervision, one of the first woodwork projects was undertaken in the new building. A farm cart was restored so that Luther, the shire-horse, could pull it round the local estate and eggs and plants on the cart could be sold. The responsibility of training Luther for this task was given to Jonathan, assisted by Joe, one of the residents of Tindall House, who had a special affinity with horses. As Joe also had a propensity for taking unscheduled naps, Luther would have to be trained to find his own way home in case Joe fell asleep at the reins!

The new workshop created up to 20 more places on the day-care scheme, offering, in theory at least, highly marketable training in carpentry, metalwork and plumbing. Although most similar training schemes were geared towards

---

18 *Leeds Weekly News*, 7 September 1995.

February 1987. As Caring For Life is launched, three of the first young men to move into Carey House join Peter Parkinson at Crag House Farm. Photograph by courtesy of the *Yorkshire Evening Post*.

The derelict properties in Meanwood which were converted into the first Tindall House in 1987.

Not a yellow brick road, but a 40-metre long pathway at Crag House
Farm created out of second-hand bricks by a young man on the Day
Care Scheme in 1993.

One of the children from Casa Bucuriei, Caring For Life's home in
Romania, enjoys riding a tricycle after an operation in England in
1993 enabled her to bend her legs for the first time.

Caring For Life goes to America! Standing on the rim of the Grand
Canyon in November 1999.

A place for reflection: a tranquil scene at the sensory pond in the Care in Creation Conservation Project at Crag House Farm.

The manager of the Floating Support Project visits a gentleman who was made homeless at the age of 65 and was re-housed by Caring For Life.

Hay-making at Crag House Farm, an important part of the Agricultural Project.

Antigone, a Yorkshire Show prize-winner from Caring For Life's herd of Old English Long Horn Cattle, appreciates a head-rub.

HRH The Countess of Wessex, Patron of Caring For Life, enjoys a conversation in front of a display of Harvest Thanksgiving donations from supporters, October 2006.

Holly, a Dales pony, is driven in the orchard at Crag House Farm, as part of the Equestrian Project.

A cuddle for a tortoiseshell, one of the many prize-winning guinea pigs bred as part of the Small Mammals Project.

A volunteer helps one of the gentlemen on the Literacy Project to hone his writing skills.

28 February 2007. Some of the first young men to be looked after by Caring For Life cut the birthday cake at the twentieth anniversary celebrations.

getting people into work within six months, this was simply not possible at Caring For Life. A recent survey of those referred to the charity had revealed that 32% were just 16 or 17 years old, that as many as 80% had been severely physically and/or sexually abused, and that 62% had learning difficulties. A growing number of these referrals had serious mental health problems and had come from psychiatric hospitals or units.[19]

While the ultimate goal might be to enable them to find paid employment, this could certainly not be achieved within six months and, for many, would never be achievable. So that the young people did not become demoralized as a result, new inducements were offered to encourage attendance at the farm. From November 1995, cooked breakfasts and lunches were provided either free of charge or at a low, subsidized cost for everyone working on the day-care schemes. Staff were amused to note a marked improvement in getting to work on time, and one young man claimed that he could smell the bacon and eggs cooking all the way along the farm lane.

The following month, a certificate scheme was introduced, allowing each person to build up a record of achievement based on targets set by their supervisor and progress judged by an independent assessor. The public presentation of certificates to proud young people who have never achieved anything before in their lives, and are sometimes touchingly overcome by emotion as they go up to receive their personal

---

19 CFL Bulletin for April/May 1995, p. 3, statistics based on the previous year's referrals.

certificates, has become one of the highlights of Caring For Life's annual Open Day. Awards are made for progress in literacy, numeracy, health and safety, but also for helpfulness, or simply for having the biggest smile on the farm. These are not meaningless soft options: for those with autism or acute depressive illnesses, it is just as much of a struggle to overcome antisocial behaviour as it is for those with learning difficulties to acquire the basics of reading and writing. The important point is that no one is overlooked and every achievement, no matter how small, is celebrated.

The expansion of the schemes at the farm was a leap of faith because it took place against a background of continuing financial hardship. Many of the grants that had helped to establish various projects, including the resettlement team, had run out. It had always been easier to find grants for new projects rather than to maintain existing ones, but the government's decision to withdraw direct funding of charities in favour of making grants through the National Lottery had a dramatic effect on Caring For Life's finances. There were two reasons for this. First and most important was the fact that Caring For Life, like many other Christian charities, had a moral objection to receiving money from what was in essence a form of legalized gambling:

We are deeply concerned that the National Lottery is entrapping some of the very needy people we are seeking to help. Many poor people are being enticed to spend money which they really do not have in the hope that ... they will win vast sums of money. Applying for money to an institution which is itself damaging some of the vulnerable people we are ministering to would be akin to seeking grants from drug barons to assist addicts who had received their drugs via those profiteering drug barons in the first place.

One of the unintended consequences of the launch of the National Lottery in November 1994 was a falling-off in public donations to charities. The attitude seemed to be that people had 'done their bit' by purchasing Lottery tickets for good causes and that there was no longer a need to give directly to charities. Caring For Life was therefore hit twice: by being unable to claim from the National Lottery and by the decline in general charitable giving. Additionally, as government funding declined, the number of applications by charities to independent sources increased, overwhelming them with paperwork and causing significant delays in disbursing money.

For Caring For Life these difficulties were compounded by a run of disasters affecting personnel. It had always been difficult to recruit and retain staff. It was a prerequisite that anyone employed by the charity had to be committed to its Christian ethos, which substantially reduced the pool of appropriately qualified people available. The wages offered could not compare with those in the private sector, making it especially difficult for those with dependent children and relatives. And it took a very special sort of person to be able to cope with the stress of being on call 24 hours a day and dealing with unpredictable young people who were often violent, abusive and suicidal. This was not a job, but a way of life. Staff shortages added to the burden of those still working and problems reached a peak in the summer of 1996. Danny Tanton, who was running the resettlement project virtually singlehanded, suffered a serious football injury that left him immobile and unable to do his job for many weeks; Geoff King, who ran the horticulture project, was suffering from stress and was away from work for several months on end. At least two other members of staff were off sick with serious long-term illnesses and two more resigned, unable to cope with the pressure of work. Sick Pay legislation meant that Caring For Life not only had to continue paying the salaries of those who were unable to work but also could not recover any of that money from the government. For the work to continue it would be essential to employ (and pay) more staff to cover the absences.

By the end of July 1996 the enormous sum of £42,000 was needed just to pay outstanding debts and salaries. An appeal to supporters explaining the crisis, and pointing out that a donation of only £1 a week extra would make all the difference, produced a flood of gifts: within a week more than £50,000 had been received from individual Christian supporters, youth groups, churches and private Christian charities. One donation came with a particularly moving message, which summed up the generosity of Caring For Life's supporters, 'My gift is just a drop in the ocean, but God can provide an ocean of drops.' This was demonstrably true: the extra £1 a week from individual supporters increased the charity's income by £8,000 a month. 'We have been truly humbled by your response,' Peter Parkinson wrote in the bulletin. 'Along with all the staff, I personally feel wholly unworthy of the love and support you have expressed for our work and ministry.'

Equally heartening was the response of some of the young people who were looked after by Caring For Life. Gary, Danny and Joe, from Tindall House, willingly assisted Jonathan with his weekend duties and undertook the heavy tasks on the farm that he was unable to do after he suffered a serious wrist injury. And Andrew, the young man who had so nearly been jailed for 20 years, began work on the resettlement team. Thrown in at the deep end, he rose to the occasion and rapidly established a close rapport with many of those whose problems he had once experienced himself.

Ingenious attempts were also made to raise money by embarking on income-generating projects. A trading company, Caring For Life Ltd, had been established in 1993, to comply with charity law. At first it had sold gardening equipment and country clothing, but this had not been particularly successful. As commissions for the specialist plasterwork dried up, Tim developed a printing business based on Caring For Life's own in-house Desk Top publishing and printing facilities, which had been used to produce the bi-monthly bulletin for supporters. This was expanded to offer a design and printing service to private clients, churches and businesses for brochures, business cards and invitations. Another new project, utilizing the skills of Chris Wilson, the mechanic who serviced the charity's cars, was vehicle maintenance. Both these projects offered the opportunity for training.

Michael, a severely disturbed but intelligent young man who had come to live in Tindall House in 1989, found his niche in the printing business, which was so successful that it had to relocate to its own dedicated office above the workshops in the new barn.

As Caring For Life limped towards the tenth anniversary of its foundation, its continuing existence seemed little short of miraculous. It is hard to imagine any other charity that could have survived such desperate straits, let alone without compromising its beliefs and vision. Christ was the rock upon which Caring For Life had been founded and he had not failed them. 'See what GOD has done' was the theme of the tenth birthday celebrations in February 1997. Reviewing the decade of ministry there was much to be thankful for: 'It is both a challenge and an encouragement to stand back and see just how much work Caring For Life has been able to do by God's grace over the past ten years,' Peter declared at the time. He went on to say:

We have housed 600 people and provided 400 of those with on-going support in terms of frequent visits, pastoral help and encouragement, and counsel. We have received a total number of 886 referrals, individuals whom we have actually been able to provide with help and counsel. We have seen 75 young people placed in full-time employment who had never worked before and we have seen 81 young people make professions of faith in Christ as a direct result of our ministry. For that we say, 'Not unto us but unto Him be all the glory.'

Yet this was not a time for complacency. He continued:

> In the past ten years we have seen some wonderful things, but the exciting figures . . . need also to be balanced by these. In the last ten years Caring For Life has opened three homes in the UK and closed down two. When we first began we had five residential places, within six months we expanded those to fifteen. These now stand at eight places.

Further analysis of the figures produced some grim statistics. Of those referred to the charity in the previous year, 45% had been 18 and under; 38% aged from 19 to 25; and only 17% over 25. Some 34.5% of them had come from temporary hostel accommodation; 22.4% had no fixed abode; 13.8% had been in custody; and 6.9% had come from psychiatric hospitals. It was when the figures were analysed to determine the underlying causes of their homelessness that the most startling statistics emerged: 52.9% had formerly been in care; 51% had a history of childhood abuse; 49% had no supportive person other than Caring For Life; 47.1% had mild to moderate learning difficulties; 41.2% were either on probation or had a history of offending; 39.2% had serious behavioural problems; 27.5% were addicted to drugs or solvents, and a further 17.6% to alcohol; 9.8% had made repeated self-harm attempts, and 5.9% suffered from a recognized psychiatric disorder.[20]

---

20 CFL Bulletin for September/October 1996, p. 5.

These statistics served to reinforce Peter's conviction as to the future direction Caring For Life should take:

> I am very conscious that we have a huge task to achieve and one of the things which is very clear to me is that the most effective work we have been able to undertake has been done with those people who have been in long-term residential care. It is through that ministry that we have seen most people come to faith in Christ and I am convinced that it is to that ministry that we must look for the future success of our work.

Never one to lack ambition on Caring For Life's behalf, Peter announced that the charity needed two new homes – one of them for young women – and that this would cost £500,000. Ironically, the latest round of Lottery bids had been specifically targeted at funding residential projects of exactly this kind, but neither the trustees nor the majority of the charity's supporters were prepared to sell their souls for tainted money. Instead, they looked to the Christian community that had been so generous and faithful in their giving over the previous decade. This was a tall order, for only two months earlier Peter had announced that Caring For Life needed to increase its regular income by £100,000 per annum just to maintain all its current projects. Even this proved impossible to find in full, despite pleas through the bulletin and presentations at churches throughout the country. The sad but simple truth was, and remains, that it is always easier to raise money for appealing babies, cute children and fluffy animals than for disturbed and unattractive adolescents whose problems society insists on believing are self-inflicted.

Around half the money needed to continue the current level of ministry was gifted or promised, and the number of those covenanting regular sums rose from 80 to between 130 and 140, but in order to secure the long-term future it was essential to reduce costs. Several staff had to be made redundant, a matter of considerable distress to all concerned as they were part of a close-knit team and many of the young people were attached to them. More than ever before it would be necessary to rely on the TFJs and other volunteers, as well as on donations in kind. The produce brought by schools and churches from their harvest festivals that year alone reduced food bills by half.

There were other problems of an entirely new kind this year. Caring For Life had always been prepared to help anyone of any background, but in the summer of 1997 a young Asian boy was referred by his school. Asif was in desperate need of help and trying to escape from a violent and unhealthy situation at home. When his family found out that Caring For Life were the agency attempting to help him, they threatened reprisals against both the staff and the farm premises. Police experts warned that the wider Muslim community would unite in trying to find the boy and that private-hire drivers, in particular, would be looking out for him. Should any such vehicle approach the farm without authorization, then police were to be called immediately. In the end Asif was unable to break away from the strong family ties of his community and was sent to Pakistan where he was beyond assistance. The one

positive outcome of this unwanted and unintentional conflict with local Muslims was that Caring For Life was brought
into very close proximity with the community constable and
policemen who responded to the emergency calls. Able to
see at first hand and for the first time the inspirational work
that the charity was doing among young offenders, the local
police force became its enthusiastic supporters.

The year 1997 had not been an easy one. At the end of it
Peter put three possible choices for the way forward to the
trustees. The first was to reduce the areas of Caring For Life's
work, maintaining only those that were commercially viable,
and accepting fewer referrals. The second was to maintain
the status quo. The third option was to take a bold step and
seek to expand the work massively, being as efficient as possible in the commercial areas, but also striving to maximize
the potential income from Christian organizations, churches
and grant-making trusts. It will perhaps not come as a sur-
prise to learn that it was the third choice that was accepted.
A new marketing/public relations/fund-raising team was appointed. Its brief included finding ways to encourage corporate sponsorship of different areas of the work and arrang-
ing for presentations to be made at Christian conferences.
The new team rapidly proved its worth, successfully targeting grant-making trusts and building up the support base
among churches. The new stream of income would make a
huge difference to the quantity and quality of the services
the charity provided. Even so, it could not live up to Peter's
blithely optimistic and ambitious plans for the future. 'We
have decided that we will move out in faith,' he announced in

December. The next year Caring For Life would try to open its first home for girls, followed in 1999 by a second home for young men and possibly a special care unit for single-parent mothers. '1998 is going to be an exciting year!'

6

Homes not Hostels

The need to open a home for young women, based on the model of Tindall House, had become increasingly urgent over the years. On average, only 25% of those referred to Caring For Life were female, but their needs were acute. Many of them were already mothers, even though they were only teenagers themselves; they came from abusive backgrounds and were living in potentially violent and dangerous situations. A typical example was a homeless 16-year-old, with a three-month-old baby, who was living, together with her boyfriend, in a council refuge. Another girl with severe learning difficulties who had been seriously abused was struggling to care for her two-month-old daughter.

Lacking basic parenting skills or a supportive family network, girls like these were at risk not only of committing abuse themselves but also of having their children removed into care. An unfortunately typical example was a young woman with learning difficulties, who had been sexually abused by her father, brothers, uncles and other men for as long as she could remember and had been taken into care at the age of 11. Placed inappropriately in a large children's home, where her vulnerability could not be protected, she fell victim to the older children who continued the abuse. When she eventually left care, aged 16, she was completely unable to cope and, in desperation, drifted back home – and back to the abuse she had fled in the first place. She had already had two children of her own when she was first referred to Caring For Life in her early twenties, but they too had been removed into care because she was unable to look after herself, let alone dependent infants.

As early as 1989, in an effort to break the cycle of abuse, Caring For Life had worked with Ruth Hanson, a research psychologist in Leeds, to devise a programme of childcare training with a Christian basis, called 'Lives in Your Hands'. Unusually, it was aimed not just at young mothers in these situations, but also at young fathers and potential fathers. This was so successful that Ruth was able to introduce the programme elsewhere in the UK. In more recent years, the day-care project had expanded to include both classes in life-skills and, under Debbie Habibzadeh's guidance, an art group where creativity was encouraged and achievement recognized.

In 1996 a YMCA national survey had discovered that one in twenty young people between the ages of 16 and 25 in Leeds were homeless and, in a reversal of previous trends, 59% of them were female. Of these girls, 54% had been forced to leave their previous accommodation because of violence and harassment. When a homeless girl came to Caring For Life, the only options available were to find her a low-rent bed-sit or a flat, which was likely to be in a run-down or unsafe area of the city, or to place her in a hostel where she would have to cook her own meals and was at risk of sexual or physical assault from other women. Most hostels had minimal staff coverage and at least 48 residents living there, yet the girls referred to Caring For Life needed individual attention and 24-hour support. Though local YWCA hostels did have 24-hour support available, only one was small enough to be able to work closely with residents.

Peter's declaration of intent to open a new home for young women had a remarkable response. Within days, over £14,000 had been donated by individual supporters; by June this had risen to £30,000 and a trust had decided to match this with a cheque of its own, but progress towards obtaining the total budgeted sum was frustratingly slow. Finding the right property was not easy either, since the remit was very precise. It needed to be in a safe and suitable area, within walking distance of basic amenities and large enough to provide ample living space for eight young women and their support staff. There was great excitement when, in the spring of 1999, the ideal house was identified in Yeadon. Not only did it have all that was required but also, most important of all, it felt like a home, with a number of cosy reception rooms where the girls could find privacy in warm and comfortable surroundings. The drawback was that it would cost more than expected. Some £140,000 had been raised by this time (including a £50,000 grant from the Henry Smith Foundation), but a further £50,000 would be needed to complete the purchase and at least £80,000 more to refurbish it to the standard required for registration.[21]

As the date for exchanging contracts approached, it became clear that the necessary sum could not be found in time. Discussing the matter with Esther and Debbie, Peter regretfully came to the decision that they would have to pull out of the purchase and together they prayed for a miracle. As they did so, they were called to the telephone in the office. Some weeks earlier, Peter and Esther had given a presentation to a handful of people in a tiny Grace Baptist church near Guildford. At the time it had seemed like a fruitless exercise, but now they learned that one of those people had decided to give Caring For Life £50,000, exactly the sum needed to buy the property. The donor was a widow who lived quietly and frugally in a small cottage; she could have spent the money on making her own life more comfortable, but she wanted to make her sacrificial gift to help others less fortunate than herself. Her remarkable generosity ensured that contracts could be exchanged on 30 July 1999 and the home for women came a step closer.

What no one had expected was the furore when the planning application for change of use was lodged. Some 48 letters of objection and a petition with 165 signatures were sent

---

21 Large grants (£25,000 and above) for the purchase and refurbishment were also given by the Harrison and Potter Trust, the Vardy Foundation and the Clothworkers' Foundation; similarly large grants towards running costs, including salaries, would be given by the Lankelly Foundation, Tudor Trust and the Esmee Fairbairn Charitable Trust.

to the council by local residents. Such was the strength of feeling that a local councillor organized a public meeting to voice the opposition and give the charity an opportunity to respond. More than 120 people crammed into the meeting and it soon became clear – at least to Peter and Esther – that the fears being expressed were unfounded. Opponents were afraid that drug addicts and offenders would be housed in premises that were close to three schools, that their presence would attract undesirable male visitors, and that the peace and quiet of the neighbourhood would be destroyed.

Peter and Esther both categorically denied that drug addicts or offenders would be housed and, in his speech, Peter tried to explain Caring For Life's vision: that this would be a long-term home for girls unable to live on their own, not a hostel for transients, that there would always be a member of staff on the premises and that the girls would spend every weekday at the farm. Although a small number of people were reassured, most remained unconvinced. 'Nothing could make me change my mind,' one local woman told the press. 'Quite a few people brought up the subject of why should it be on our doorstep and be in the middle of a residential estate? I am sure there must be other places.'[22]

The public reaction was disappointing, though understandable. 'I have come to believe that where God blesses the most, opposition will always be the fiercest,' Peter wrote after the meeting. 'Certainly all of us who are Christians will be

---

22 *Wharfe Valley Times*, 11 November 1999; *Wharfedale & Airedale Observer*, 25 November 1999, p. 5; *Yorkshire Evening Post*, 22 November 1999.

very conscious that there is never a victory without a battle and no battle is easily won.' There was some small comfort in the fact that Tindall House had also faced opposition in the beginning, but that local people there had become supporters once experience had proved their fears groundless. And the unwanted publicity had not been entirely negative. As a result of reading about the controversy in the papers, one local woman rang Caring For Life to say that she was desperate for help for her daughter and, until then, had never heard of the charity whose aid she now sought.

Planning permission was finally granted in November 1999, but this was only the beginning of an uphill struggle to open the home. To ensure that threats against the property did not materialize, Tim Parkinson and one of the TFJs, Martyn Smith, took up residence and installed security gates at the end of the drive. On their last night in the house, they discovered that the cellar was waist-high in foul water and had to call out the fire brigade. Having invested much time and effort in attempting to build relationships with the neighbours, Tim and Martyn were dismayed when the firemen started an extremely noisy engine at 1 a.m. and spent the next two hours pumping out the water – straight into the adjoining gardens.

More seriously, Environmental Health and Fire Safety officers demanded alterations that risked creating not only a more institutionalized atmosphere but also claustrophobic closed-in areas that would inevitably make damaged young women feel anxious. The alternative was to install a sprinkler system – actually a more desirable option since it meant that in the event of a fire the girls could remain in their rooms instead of having to be evacuated altogether by a single member of staff. Unfortunately, it added a further £8,500 to costs, which were already spiralling. And plans to complete the conversion in two stages, allowing the first four girls to move in as soon as possible, were quashed by the local authority on safety grounds. This meant that an additional £100,000 would have to be raised before any referrals could be accepted at all.

This was just beyond Caring For Life's means. As yet another new year dawned without the prospect of the home opening, Peter and Esther decided to make a last-ditch appeal to the Fire Safety officer. Was there any way he could permit the first phase of the home to open? Much to their astonishment, he agreed, on condition that a new water main was installed to the house to service the fire safety installations. Unfortunately, there was not enough money available even to pay for this. Then, in one of those miraculous turns of events that the charity had experienced so often before, the next day Peter and Esther went to see a company that was considering supporting Caring For Life:

> We went to see them and they asked what were the things, right now, that we most urgently needed. I immediately mentioned the need for the new water main . . . Incredibly they turned out to be the very company of contractors which Yorkshire Water would use to do this costly work. At that first meeting with us the Chairman picked up his phone, had a five minute conversation with Yorkshire

Water and said to us – 'Consider it done! We will install the pipe! Now, what else?' Esther and I were absolutely speechless. For us that was two miracles in two days!!

On 3 March 2001, three years later than planned, Wendy Margaret Home was officially opened in a quiet family ceremony. The family was that of Wendy Brownnutt, after whom it had been named. As Wendy Pollard, before her marriage, she had worked with Esther at Foxcroft Children's Home, had been one of the original founders of Caring For Life, and worked as one of the first supervisors at Tindall House. In 1998 she had become pregnant for the first time, only to be diagnosed with terminal cancer. Her condition deteriorated so rapidly that her consultant decided to deliver her baby boy prematurely; weighing less than five pounds, he had to stay in hospital for seven weeks, but his prognosis was good. Despite undergoing intensive courses of chemotherapy, however, there was no hope for his mother. Wendy died in her sleep on 8 January 1999, four months after giving birth to her son, and her funeral was attended by many of the young people to whom she had been such a devoted friend over so many years. Her Christian faith and her central role in starting Caring For Life would be commemorated by naming the new home for girls after her.

The first two girls, Susie and Kate, moved into Wendy Margaret Home on 26 April, followed three weeks later by a third, Christine. Susie was just 21, but had lived in more than 50 different homes and made many attempts to kill herself. The previous November she had taken a massive overdose and was technically dead on arrival at Leeds General Infirmary. The Accident and Emergency team had opened up her chest and physically massaged her heart back into beating again. For five days it was touch and go whether she lived or died – and when she regained consciousness she cursed the doctors for saving her life. Everyone expected her to make another suicide attempt, so when she was moved from the medical ward it was into a psychiatric ward. There her liaison social worker, who had first referred someone to Caring For Life 14 years earlier, decided that her only chance of surviving was to be taken into the charity's care. Susie was invited to Crag House Farm for an introductory visit and at the end of the first day confided to Esther, 'I was going to kill myself last night, but I decided that I would go up to the farm to see what the people were like. I think God stopped me killing myself. Esther, I think he is giving me another chance.' (Kate had a slightly different view of her first visit to the farm, remarking, with unintentional humour, 'I don't want to go to the funny farm!')

Susie, however, loved the farm and settled in very quickly. A few days later she celebrated her twenty-first birthday there with a small party and surprised everyone by asking to make a speech. She simply said, 'Thank you for taking me in, I now have a new family and a reason for living.'

The realization of the dream to open a home for girls did not mean that Tindall House was neglected. For some years there had been a settled group of young men living there, including seven of the eight who are still in residence today. (The final member, David, joined them in 1998.) As Dave

Skidmore, the supervisor, noted in April of that year, their average age was fast approaching 28, and, having lived together for so many years, they had learnt to relate well to each other. The settled routine and happy atmosphere were threatened by two events that summer. Dave decided after several years at Tindall House that he wanted to take a masters degree in social work and left at the end of August. It took some time to find a suitable replacement, but one of the TFJs, Gareth Carey-Jones, the son of Caring For Life's first treasurer, applied for the post. Interviewed by the residents of Tindall House themselves, as well as the staff, he won their seal of approval and took up office just before Christmas.

Dave's departure also coincided with the enforced removal of one of the young men. Antony, one of the first residents who had made remarkable progress since his arrival, mute and in handcuffs, in 1988, had been convicted of theft. Having bought a number of presents in preparation for Christmas, he ran out of money and stole some CDs from a student house. Appearing before the same judge who had recommended that Brian and Andrew serve life sentences for arson, Antony was sentenced to eight months in prison and spent Christmas in Armley jail. It was a horrific experience for him – like many of those with his degree of autism, he was subjected to verbal and physical assaults from other inmates that threatened to undermine all the progress he had made in Caring For Life's care – but he clung to his faith and in the first few months alone received more than 90 letters from staff, his fellow young people and supporters. His friends at Tindall House insisted that his birthday and

Christmas presents should be saved for his return in March and his place in the home was also kept open for him. This had been the Caring For Life promise, but it was not without adverse consequences for the charity: only a retainer for Antony's housing benefit was paid while he was in prison, putting considerable strain on the home's finances.

With these changes taking place and the focus of so much attention on the new home for women, it was important not to make the men at Tindall House feel sidelined or forgotten. The windows of the home had long needed replacing, but grants from trusts and the Dulux Community Projects Scheme enabled the whole property to be double-glazed and re-painted throughout in colour schemes chosen by the men themselves. Fund-raising events held by, among others, a Leeds city centre store, and a group of staff and volunteers who completed a sponsored climb of the three peaks in the Yorkshire Dales, raised enough money to carry out further refurbishments, including the laundry and kitchen improvements.

Morale at Tindall House was also boosted by the trip of a lifetime. Ever since Caring For Life had first opened its doors, it had been a tradition for those living in the home to take an annual holiday together. For many years this had been a trip to Center Parcs during the first week in January, the chalet-style accommodation providing the privacy needed by damaged and vulnerable young men, and the sporting facilities offering an opportunity to relax and let off steam. In 1994 four of the young men, accompanied by two members of staff, had enjoyed a week's holiday in France as guests of the charity's supporters. The visit had been an enormous success, with trips to Paris and the beach, and Antony displaying a hitherto unsuspected gift for languages when negotiating the local supermarkets.

Now, however, a much more ambitious holiday was in the offing. Mike Castle,[23] a close friend of Peter's and a generous supporter of Caring For Life, who lived in Los Angeles, invited all the Tindall House residents to visit the USA. Since most of them would need one-to-one care on the holiday, and everyone had to pay for themselves, this was something of a challenge. Even though Danny chose to remain at home, enough staff had to be found who were willing and able to accompany the seven men who wanted to go. Most of them had never been abroad before, but the desire to do so gave them the motivation and discipline to save up gradually for the trip and, as the date of their flights drew near, anticipation reached fever pitch.

On 1 November 1999 the party set off for California and immediately encountered their first hitch. Five minutes into the 12-hour flight from Heathrow to Los Angeles, David, an autistic man who had never flown anywhere before, discovered he was afraid of flying and decided to get off. He eventually managed to get through the flight, but only with a great deal of reassurance from two members of Caring For Life's staff who had to sit beside him and hold his hands all the way. As they later remarked, any other passengers with

---

23 At the end of 2006 Caring For Life was registered as a Non-Profit Organization in the USA and Mike Castle became the charity's first Director of Operations in the USA.

a nervous disposition could not have been helped by David asking everyone who walked past him down the aisle, 'Do you think we are going to crash? Are we going to die?'

Arriving in Los Angeles, the group was given a tremendous welcome and wonderful hospitality by Mike Castle and his wife, who escorted them to Disneyland, Hollywood, Las Vegas, the Grand Canyon, Death Valley and Yosemite National Park. It was perhaps typical that Joe, who loved working with the animals at Crag House Farm, would describe his favourite moment of the holiday as seeing the 'special goats' (actually very rare big-horned sheep) in Titus Canyon on the way to Death Valley. For Gary, a devotee of American films and television programmes, it was seeing the Hollywood sign and John Wayne's star on the Walk of Fame pavement on Hollywood Boulevard. This was surprising, perhaps, as his ultimate experience ought to have been his visit to the Coca-Cola shop in Las Vegas, since he was an avid collector of anything to do with the drink. The shop was not only shaped like a Coca-Cola bottle, but also sold every imaginable variant of memorabilia. With 200 painstakingly saved dollars in his pocket preserved for this very moment, Gary found himself paralysed by the abundance of choice. Knowing how much he had looked forward to this opportunity, Peter tried to persuade him to buy something as a memento. Gary eventually left with a fridge magnet that had only cost a few cents – and Peter had to spend several hours the next day scouring shops on Gary's behalf for a Coca-Cola car to make up for the disappointment.

It was inevitable that being in strange surroundings would cause difficulties for men whose ordinary daily lives were a struggle. Peter remembers one particular incident in Yosemite National Park which was both poignant and funny. Michael, who suffers from acute psychological problems caused by childhood abuse and easily loses his temper, is also afraid of steps, slopes and slippery or shiny surfaces. The group had been to see the giant Sequoia trees and the way back to the minibus took them down a long sloping pathway which was also icy in places. While the rest of the group forged ahead, Michael was left behind, edging slowly and painfully step by step down the hill. Despite being offered lots of help, he was extremely nervous and, as he always did in such circumstances, became increasingly belligerent and foul-mouthed. In an attempt to encourage him to move a little faster, Peter said to him, 'Come on, Michael, there are bears in these woods,' to which he received the incomparable reply, 'I'd rather be eaten by a bear than walk down this hill!'

That Michael was able to do this at all was little short of a miracle. Earlier in the summer, he had gone through a traumatic experience. Partly as a result of having 13 spoonfuls of sugar in his coffee, his teeth had deteriorated to the point that they had become blackened stumps. He regularly suffered from infected gums and abscesses but, despite the excruciating pain, he was too frightened to see a dentist or doctor. The task of convincing him that this was absolutely necessary fell to Tim Parkinson, who had developed a close bond working with Michael on the printing project. It took months of persuasion, but eventually he agreed that something had to be done. Arriving at the dentist, the first thing to confront him was a shiny floor and, shaking with nerves, and with

Tim supporting him on one side and Dave Skidmore on the other, he had to be coaxed inch by inch into the consulting room. It took a mere ten seconds for the dentist to see that all Michael's teeth would have to be removed, but a few months later the phobia of shiny floors had to be confronted again as Michael was booked into Leeds General Infirmary for the operation. Foreseeing the problem, Tim had brought him an hour earlier than necessary, observing that 'it was quite funny watching people's faces as they turned the corner to see Michael gripping my arm, extremely tightly, cursing at the floor, with me just standing there acting as if it was all normal'. Having seen him safely delivered to the ward, Tim spent a sleepless night worrying that Michael would panic and become abusive or confrontational because he was frightened. Returning at 8 o'clock on the dot the next morning, he was somewhat non-plussed to find Michael lying in bed, grinning broadly and declaring that 'nurses are great'.

It was not until Tim accompanied him down to the operating room that problems really began. Although the anaesthetics team did their best to reassure him, Michael was terrified by the unfamiliar clinical surroundings and procedures and, when his wrist was wiped in preparation for the needle, he lost all control. Kicking out at all those round him, he tried to jump off the table. Tim, who had been holding his hand throughout, tried to calm him down, but in the end it was decided that the only way to proceed was to administer some 'strawberry smelling' gas. Since the mask could not be put directly on his face, it had to be held a few inches above – which meant that Tim, who was also only a few inches away, unintentionally received the same dose. As Michael gradually became more relaxed and faint, so did Tim, only just tearing himself away before he passed out as Michael fell asleep.

After the operation, Tim was brought into the recovery room to be there when Michael came round from the anaesthetic. When he finally opened his eyes, Tim asked him if he was all right, and received a 'thumbs-up' sign, but a few moments later Michael did something totally unexpected. Removing his oxygen mask from his sore and bleeding mouth he whispered, 'Tim'. Tim replied, 'Yes, Michael?' 'Tim, are you still my friend?' he asked. Although Tim immediately replied, 'Michael, of course I am. I'm proud of you. Of course we're still friends, we're brothers. Well done!' he was profoundly moved. Michael, like many with his condition, had never before given a hint that he cared for someone other than himself. At this critical and life-changing moment, when he had climbed a huge hurdle in his life and had the operation that he had never thought he would have the courage to do, he needed the reassurance that some things would not change. When he needed a friend, that friend would be there. And that, as Tim says, sums up exactly the ethos of Caring For Life.

7

Hand to Mouth

Hand in hand with all the developments taking place at the residential homes was a major expansion of the facilities at Crag House Farm. This was due in part to the need to generate more income. It had always been the case that the various day-care schemes were meant to be self-financing, so that the whole project would not be put in jeopardy if one of them should fail. But there was also always pressure to increase the number of places available, so that more young people could benefit from the therapeutic activities on offer. It was therefore important to make the most of the farm's assets and exploit its commercial potential to the full. Free-range egg production had always been one of Caring For Life's most successful business ventures, so it made sense to increase the size of the egg-laying flock. In a typical example of one project offering practical support to another, the young men working under Rob's guidance in the workshop assisted in refurbishing the old hen houses and building four new ones. The size of the flock was increased from some 350 birds to over 1,000 in six months and weekly egg production rose from 150 dozen the previous year to almost 500 dozen by the middle of 1998. By the end of the year there would be 1,600 birds producing around 700 dozen eggs weekly, all of which were cleaned, graded and boxed on site by the young people in preparation for sale through a local supermarket chain. Despite the increase in production, the hens were still free-range and reared to the highest animal welfare standards, winning the RSPCA's Freedom Food accreditation, and demonstrating that the charity cared for life in all its forms.

A second major area of expansion was made possible by the generosity of a supporter who bought 55 acres of land adjoining the farm and gave it to the charity. This transformed the agricultural project, relieving pressure on grazing land and increasing by five times the acreage of hay meadow available, so that it would no longer be necessary to purchase hay to feed the stock through the winter. The rest of the land, which extended down a steep valley side to the beck in the bottom, was earmarked for a new conservation project. By planting trees, restoring hedgerows and re-opening the original farm fishponds it was hoped that native wildlife would be tempted back into the area, creating a tranquil and beautiful retreat for the troubled young people to enjoy. The scheme had to be entirely funded from grants and dedicated donations, so as not to encroach on money needed for Caring For Life's other core projects, but ultimately it too was intended to make a financial contribution towards the charity's crucial work.

Initially disappointed of the hoped-for grant from the new landfill tax, which would have enabled work to begin immediately, the project had to be shelved for another year, but by the summer of 2000 the basic work had been completed. Contractors with earth-moving vehicles had moved literally tons of soil, rubble and clay to create paths and ponds, clear streams and ditches. Now a gently meandering path led down the hillside, past a restored medieval pond where mallards and moorhens were already nesting and by a smaller invertebrate pond specially created to provide a habitat for newts, frogs and toads. One side of the path was planted with a fragrant lavender hedge and the other with a raised bed built in old Yorkshire stone to form a lemon-scented garden. Through the trees were other raised scented gardens, accessible for wheelchair users, containing a variety of fragrant leaves and flowers. A textured garden, containing tactile materials such as stones, bark, soft grasses, woolly leaves and ferns, was created within a circular stone bed and, elsewhere, a fountain falling on stones was planted round with moisture-loving plants and shrubs. The path wound down past a new sensory pond planted with reeds, yellow flag, water lilies and other aquatic plants, beside a stream with shallow areas dug out for small mammals and birds such as curlews, and across a restored waterway to the two largest ponds dug out of the valley bottom.

The combination of water – deep, shallow, standing and running – trees, shrubs and meadow grasslands proved to be a magnet for wildlife of all kinds from the very first. The addition of nesting boxes and bird feeders, made in the workshops, added to the attraction. The whole valley was soon alive with the sound of small birdsong as well as the haunting cries of curlew, lapwing, skylarks and owls; the observant could catch the brilliant flash of kingfishers over the ponds, the splash of a water vole slipping into the beck, or the lazy circling of red kite riding the updraughts. Brown hares in the fields were joined by deer, badgers and otters, as well as an enormous variety of small mammals and amphibians. Creating and maintaining the habitats to encourage these birds and animals to flourish would become a full-time occupation for many of the young people working at the farm. Most of them had never experienced anything but an urban environment, and it was a revelation to them to see the emergent beauty of God's natural creation. Spotting and identifying the latest new arrival became, and remains, a matter of pride and excitement, but it is also extremely competitive: Alan, a young man with severe learning difficulties who lives at Tindall House, was overjoyed to have seen the first golden oriole – a confirmed sighting – but later claimed to have seen a '40-metre dragonfly' and a toucan!

It was always intended that the conservation project would be open to visitors: the sensory gardens, in particular, had been designed and created with the needs of the blind, deaf and wheelchair-bound in mind. The elderly, too, would benefit in ways that could not have been imagined. One lady with Alzheimer's disease was brought by her daughter: unable to remember anything about her own life or even recognize members of her close family, she was able to identify the scents of the herb garden and talk knowledgeably and coherently about them. For her daughter it was a last and highly emotional glimpse of the woman her mother had once been, made all the more poignant by the fact that she died not long afterwards. The 'conversation project', as some of the young people mistakenly – but appropriately – called it, was also an ideal opportunity for those who had been helped themselves to help others, guiding visitors round the gardens, pointing out the wildlife, and serving them cream teas afterwards.

The expansion of the farm activities and the financial imperative to raise the public profile of Caring For Life led naturally to a decision to take a stand at the Great Yorkshire Show. This huge annual event, held over three consecutive days in July on a permanent site just outside Harrogate, is a celebration of the region's countryside and farming and a showcase for the best local produce from livestock to table. Caring For Life's stand in the agricultural section proved an enormous success from its very first outing in 1998. Manned by some of the young people, as well as staff and volunteers, it attracted several thousand people, drawn in ostensibly by the opportunity to see some of the rare breeds from the farm but also, as cynics would admit, by the offer of free coffee or orange juice and a quiet place to sit down away from the heat and crush of the crowds.

The unusual nature of the stand meant that media interest was also high, particularly the following year when the stand included an ambitious feature on the conservation project, complete with pond, waterfall, trees, plants and live birds of prey. This resulted in a feature on Crag House Farm, including the annual harvest, on the BBC's *Songs of Praise* programme – despite the fact that Misty the barn owl disgraced herself during filming by attacking the fluffy sound boom hovering over her head – and on BBC Radio 4's *Changing Places*. It also led to a flood of newspaper articles, covering the launch of the conservation project and lauding the many groups of volunteers from local and national companies who gave their time and labour to help the staff and young people to clear the land and plant trees, hedges and bulbs.

One of the many visitors to Crag House Farm was the well-known gardener, Geoffrey Smith, a veteran of the BBC's *Gardener's Question Time*, who for 20 years had been superintendent of the Northern Horticultural Society's botanical gardens at Harlow Carr, near Harrogate. Like so many others who have been drawn accidentally into the Caring For Life ambit, he became an immediate and enthusiastic supporter, offering his expert advice and active assistance in creating the conservation project. When it was officially opened to the public at Caring For Life's Millennium Open Day, Geoffrey Smith and Pat Clegg, who had played a major role in bringing the project to fruition, were the natural choice to do the honours. More than 1,000 people gathered to watch them do so and to hear speeches by the Lord Mayor of Leeds, Councillor Bernard Atha, and by two local MPs, David Hinchliffe and Harold Best, who had jointly hosted a reception celebrating the work of Caring For Life in the House of Commons the previous year. Harold Best had then described the charity as being 'at the heart of my constituency both in geographical terms and as practical inspiration'.

As Christmas approached in the year 2000, it seemed that

Caring For Life had really turned a corner and the future looked bright. The resettlement team received a large grant from the Lloyds TSB Foundation to help fund their work, the Resource Centre had been completely renovated with a new floor, ceiling, window frames and walls by 20 volunteers from the local Asda store, and Wendy Margaret Home was about to open its doors to its first women residents. Then disaster struck. Caring For Life needed £750,000 a year just to maintain its pastoral work but, unlike many other charities, it did not have significant resources held in abeyance as a contingency fund. It had always been the case, as Peter put it, that 'we are in a very real way living day to day from hand to mouth'. The only way forward for the ministry was by faith and, so far, God and his servants had always provided. But as the staff prepared food hampers and Christmas presents to give to around 100 people they supported in the community, their own salaries were not being paid in full. 'We never have very much lee way, in terms of financial flexibility,' Peter explained in the monthly bulletin to supporters, 'but inexplicably our income for the last two months has been much lower than usual.'

Ironically, the reason for this may have been all the publicity given to recent grants and donations: though these were earmarked for specific projects, they created a general impression of a healthy income that might have led ordinary supporters to believe that their own contributions were no longer necessary. Nothing could have been further from the truth – which was that the steady weekly and monthly giving by faithful supporters in churches and Christian groups throughout the country was, and is, the mainstay of the charity. Some 55% of Caring For Life's total income regularly comes from supporters.[24]

Though this was not the first time staff had had to forgo their salaries – and what other organization could have asked for and received such a sacrifice? – it was an uncomfortable and worrying situation, especially for those with children and dependent families. The young people who relied so heavily on Caring For Life were also deeply affected. Wilf, who had less money than any other resident of Tindall House, offered to give a sum each week to help pay the staff, saying that they had given so much to him that he wanted to give something back to them. Another young man with severe physical disabilities and a speech impediment, who travelled many miles each day to attend the day-care scheme, had only recently become a Christian, but his touching faith that all would be well was an inspiration to all. Earlier in the year the college he attended had prohibited him from going to the farm on health and safety grounds. Because he dragged his feet as he pulled himself along on his crutches, his special safety boots had worn out more quickly than expected. There was no money to replace them so, to his great distress, he was not allowed to go to the farm.

When Peter told this story the next day at a church in Houghton-le-Spring, County Durham, the congregation

---

24 In 1999 this compared to only 24% from trusts, a mere 4% from the government, 11% from residential income, and 6% from commercial activity: CFL Millennium Bulletin, p. 6.

held a spontaneous collection and raised enough money to pay for another pair. Deeply moved that Christian people whom he had never met cared enough about him to do such a thing, Danny had taken the first tentative steps towards baptism. Now, in faith, he stammered out his own prayer: 'We are doing your work, Lord, please help us, you can't let us down!' And, once again, God did not fail those who put their trust in him. A generous response from supporters ensured that enough money was received to pay the salaries in full just in time for Christmas.

This crisis, however, was as nothing compared to the one about to strike. The millennium year came to an end and a new year began with sub-zero temperatures that iced over the ponds and brought heavy falls of snow which lay on the frozen ground for weeks at a time. And then in February 2001 an outbreak of foot-and-mouth disease was reported in pigs at an abattoir in Essex. The European Union acted immediately, banning all British milk, meat and livestock exports the day after the first reported case, but a series of catastrophic errors by the British government turned a crisis into a disaster. The Ministry for Agriculture, Fisheries and Farming failed not only to appreciate that the disease affected sheep and cattle, as well as pigs, but also to implement an immediate ban on the movement of farm animals, to use vaccination to ring-fence affected areas and to bring in the army to control the outbreak until it was too late. As a result the disease spread rapidly, almost 4 million animals were slaughtered, including newborn calves and lambs, and the livelihoods of thousands of farmers were destroyed. The cost to the rural economy and tourism was estimated at £5 billion.[25]

On Friday 23 March, Caring For Life received the official telephone call that everyone had dreaded. A farm just under two miles away had a confirmed outbreak of the disease and Crag House Farm was now within an infected area. Unable to get a clear answer as to what this meant in terms of keeping the farm open to those who worked on the day-care projects, the Executive Committee held an emergency meeting and decided to suspend all activities at the farm until advice had been received from the ministry vet and procedures had been agreed with MAFF which would enable operations to continue.

At 4.30 that afternoon, Peter and Esther called everyone together and told them the terrible news. Even the staff were not prepared for the devastating effect that this would have on the young people, especially those who had worked on the farm for many years. Joe broke down in tears at the thought that he would not be able to look after his beloved horses and, worse still, might never see them again. Gary and Danny were equally devastated, not least because many of the sheep they cared for were imminently due to lamb and all might have to be culled. One of the girls on the day-care project, who was almost blind, burst out crying: 'You mustn't stop me coming here,' she sobbed, 'this is my home! What shall I do if I can't come here? I have nowhere else! I have nowhere else!' Antony, who repeats himself endlessly when agitated,

---

25 www.news.bbc.co.uk.

also became very distressed, muttering, 'We come here! We come here every day! They can't stop us coming here! This is where we belong! I work here! They can't stop me coming here!' Although the staff had known, of course, that the farm meant a lot to the young people, it was utterly overwhelming to hear so many of them express its importance in their lives so vividly and powerfully.

The men from Tindall House were tense and upset on their journey home. Arguments flared between them and, uncharacteristically, one between Joe and Michael almost came to blows. When they got home they all went off to their own rooms, but then Danny asked the supervisor if he would pray with him that the farm might be spared foot-and-mouth disease. Thinking that it would be good to give the others a chance to join in, the supervisor informed them all that there would be a prayer meeting in the lounge and was astounded when all six who were in at the time came downstairs. After a few short and sincere prayers that God would protect Caring For Life were said, there was a few seconds' silence, then Joe beckoned to Michael, walked over and gave him an enormous hug. It was an infinitely touching and selfless gesture of reconciliation and goodwill in a fraught situation: a glimpse of God among the tears.

The next day the official restriction order arrived, followed a day later by the MAFF vet. Jonathan Parkinson, with whom the responsibility for the livestock ultimately rested, had even considered asking whether to volunteer that all the animals should go for slaughter, in a bid to ensure that at least the young people could get back to the farm as soon as possible. On second thoughts, however, he realized that the consequences of such a decision on those who actually cared for the animals on a daily basis would be too traumatic. The time might come when the livestock would all be condemned to slaughter, but it was better that that decision was taken out of Caring For Life's own hands.

The MAFF vet's inspection revealed that all the animals on the farm were free of foot-and-mouth, but a 5-mile animal movement exclusion order was imposed until further notice. The vet would continue to visit regularly to check that the stock remained disease-free and insisted that, in the circumstances, a special licence would have to be obtained before the charity could continue to sell its free-range eggs. Since the income from the eggs had recently doubled and was crucial for covering the cost of the farm equipment, it was critically important to ensure that a licence was obtained, a process that the vet assured them would not be a problem.

On Monday morning, Jonathan began the long and frustrating process of trying to negotiate with MAFF officials. Telephone call followed telephone call as he was passed from one person to the next and it was only when he eventually became so insistent and forceful that he could not be ignored that he was informed that a decision would be taken. Feeling physically sick as the fate of the farm hung in the balance, he had to wait another three hours before he was finally told that he had got his licence.

It was also only by being doggedly tenacious and insistent about the importance of allowing the young people to return to the farm that he finally wrung concessions out of MAFF.

The terms were very exacting: transport to and from the farm was to be strictly limited; no new people could be taken on to the day-care schemes; everyone was to wear fully waterproof clothing that could be washed off; disinfectant foot baths had to be used, and a rigid code of practice observed to control and reduce the risk of infection. The donation of a minibus at this difficult time was an amazing answer to prayer, enabling the young people to be picked up at various locations and brought to the farm, instead of making their own way there independently. For some of them, this meant a much longer day than they were accustomed to, but they were all so eager to be at the farm that they coped quite happily with the change. A local church, Cookridge Methodist, allowed the staff to leave their cars in its car park during the day so that they too could all be taken to the farm in the single minibus, while the resettlement team temporarily relocated its office to the home of one of its staff.

On Tuesday 27 March, the young people were able to return 'home' to the farm. It was a joyous occasion, despite the difficulties in getting there and the 'spacesuits' they were all obliged to wear. Peter was able to share with them the extraordinarily relevant daily Bible readings that had been set for Leeds Reformed Baptist Church that week. The Monday reading had been Psalm 36, which included the verses:

Thy steadfast love, O Lord, extends to the heavens, thy faithfulness to the clouds. Thy righteousness is like the mountains of God, thy judgments are like the great deep; man and beast thou savest, O Lord (vv. 5–6).

The reading for that day, Tuesday, was Psalm 37, where verse 3 proclaimed: 'Trust in the Lord, and do good; so you will dwell in the land, and enjoy security.' 'Sometimes I find God whispers to me,' Peter told them, 'sometimes he shouts!'

Although the farm escaped an outbreak of foot-and-mouth, the financial consequences of the epidemic were disastrous. The farm had to be closed to all visitors, which meant the enforced cancellation of the annual Open Day, supporters' days and various fund-raising sales. One plant sales day went ahead, and that only because Cookridge Methodist Church hosted the event; although it enabled some of the plants grown for sale to be sold, transporting them from the farm was extremely difficult and impractical. Less obviously, the closure of the farm to the public also impacted on income from potential supporters too, as grant-making trusts, church groups and other bodies were unable to visit the heart of Caring For Life. As a direct consequence of the disease, the charity lost at least £85,000 of its annual income. Although it seemed that every conceivable obstacle was being put in the way of the charity's survival, there were some positive aspects to the crisis. Jonathan, for instance, was able to help a farming neighbour, who was in financial difficulties, by making her silage for her free of charge.

And the young people themselves were drawn closer by a sense of shared trouble. The staff were extremely moved to discover that Antony had bought a thoughtful present for the girl who was almost blind – a cassette recording of the New Testament. And the men from Tindall House rallied protectively round Danny when news came that his father had died suddenly and unexpectedly.

The staff also did everything possible to keep morale high, organizing a series of activities designed to give those in their care a break from the tedious routines imposed by disease-control, including trips to the coast, sports days, barbecues and overnight camping in the valley of the conservation project. Deprived of the chance to mix with supporters at Open Days, many of them took the opportunity to express their appreciation of all that Caring For Life had done for them in a special issue of the bulletin. Seventeen-year-old Lucy was pregnant and living in a hostel when she first met Anita from the resettlement team:

> I knew where I wanted to go with my life but I just needed some help to get there. I saw Anita a few times – it was great because she was never like a worker, she was more of a friend. All I want in life is to be settled and to try to be an excellent mother. I've moved now and feel better where I am. I'm doing a mother and baby course and it's brilliant. I'm going for all of my exams that I missed at school because of bullying. I'm glad my life has changed for the best.

One young man, who had been coming to the farm for about eight months, loved working on the conservation and agriculture projects, but admitted, 'I also like being in a place where people care for me even when I'm a pain in the neck.' Bobby, too, a very poorly man who rarely dared to leave his home, had attended the day-care projects several days a week for three years and worked with the birds of prey for nine months. 'Being a disabled person, this was my first full day's work for twenty years!' he proudly declared. 'I have especially enjoyed special things like being dragged through the snow on a sledge! I was shouting "Faster! Faster!" but I don't think you could get more than ten miles per hour out of it! I have never worked with such good people.'

Even though the foot-and-mouth crisis gradually eased and normal activities on the farm began to resume, the run of calamities continued. The terrible television pictures of the terrorist attack on the Twin Towers in New York deeply distressed and frightened the young people. 'The news has really upset me,' Michael wrote, 'I know my family weren't hurt, but I'm still upset because we've got a lot of supporters in America. I'm glad some people got out alive.' 'I have found everything quite worrying,' Wilf added. 'I don't know why they have done that, it's very confusing. It has made me pray a lot more.' For Joe the events were especially traumatic because he was extremely sensitive about his parentage. His father was a Muslim and had tried to force Joe to become one too. When Joe refused, his father had thrown him out of the house, even though he was only a teenager and suffered from severe learning difficulties. For a month Joe had lived on the streets, sleeping in parks, market stalls and bus shelters, until Caring For Life had taken him in. He had become a Christian and since then his father had never spoken to him or looked at him, even crossing the street to avoid doing so. Despite having been a much-loved member of the Caring For Life family for many years, the fact that Muslim extremists had carried out the attack made him afraid that he would be rejected because of his Muslim background and he needed much reassurance.

Closer to home, but equally disturbing, was the fact that Susie moved out of Wendy Margaret Home after just six months; although she continued to attend the day-care project for a while, it was clear that she was drifting away and by the end of the year she had left Leeds altogether. Although Caring For Life feared that she would return to her old abusive habits and be lost to both the charity and herself, she has remained in touch and continues to do reasonably well.

Worse still, on 12 November, one of Caring For Life's most vulnerable ladies was found dead in her home. Jane was 47 and, among her other problems, had suffered from mental illness in recent years. In the five years of her association with Caring For Life she had changed from being aggressive, unpleasant and rude into a quiet and shy lady who loved being at the farm so much that she would laugh, sing and dance as she worked in the poly-tunnels. That morning she had been due to come to the farm, but the home care agency alerted the community nurse that no answer could be obtained at her house. Esther tried to ring to see if she was all right, but there was no reply. Esther and Peter rushed to join the nurse at Jane's house, only to find her lying by the bed where she had died. A forensic investigation revealed that she had accidentally set her clothes alight while cooking herself a meal, taken off her burnt clothing in the bathroom, covered herself with wet towels, and then gone to bed. Later she had got out of bed and lain down on the floor where she had died. She had suffered 85% burns and would not have survived, even if she had been taken to hospital, but that did not lessen the burden of sorrow and self-recrimination. The only small comfort was that the night before she died, Jane had attended a service at Leeds Reformed Baptist Church at which one of the texts was 2 Timothy 4.16–17, describing how Paul had been alone, deserted by everyone, but God had stood by him. Peter had explained that there are times when terrible things may happen, and we may feel alone, but that Jesus is always with us: 'We even applied this to the fact that one day we will die, and if Jesus is our Saviour and our Lord he will be there too.' Jane, as always, had listened attentively.

Telling the staff and young people at Caring For Life of Jane's death in such tragic circumstances was extremely difficult. Many burst into tears, including Kate, who had been one of Jane's closest friends. As Peter told them the news, it suddenly began to rain heavily, and Kate said, 'When I was a little girl my mum said that when it rained it was because God was crying. I think he is crying with us now, because of Jane.'

8

A Time of Miracles

Caring For Life had survived the foot-and-mouth crisis, but only just: despite many generous gifts of cash to help with the additional expenses of purchasing protective clothing, new Wellingtons and disinfectant, one month there was only £2 to spare after paying the staff salaries. If nothing else, it was at least proof that every pound donated by supporters really mattered. The enforced isolation of the farm had, however, enabled a rearrangement and refurbishment to take place: new offices had been created above the workshop and a new telephone system installed, enabling Michael to develop a whole new set of skills – not always appreciated by unwary callers – as the temporary Caring for Life receptionist.

In November 2001 a new day-care facility opened. Housed in the former offices, it proved remarkably popular, not least because it was a warm refuge from the cold, wind and driving rain of a typical Yorkshire winter. The idea was that the new range of arts and crafts activities, supervised by Debbie, would be available two days a week to all those who attended the farm. They were designed to expand their interests, broaden their skills, stimulate their creativity and increase their enjoyment of life, their appreciation of the wonder of God's creation and their sense of personal fulfilment. One of the first products of the new scheme was a very special fresh flower and foliage wreath for Jane's funeral, made from plants in the sensory gardens where she had worked. Normally, however, the emphasis would be on seasonal projects. In the run-up to Christmas, for instance, the men and women would make Christmas cakes, cards, table decorations and gifts. Making the most of the opportunities provided by the conservation scheme, there would also be sketching of winter landscapes, creating collages from natural autumnal materials, and studying winter light and colours.

Despite the atrocious weather, winter was the ideal time to plant trees – at least as far as the trees were concerned. Staff, volunteers and the young people themselves worked hard, planting out 2,800 hedgerow trees between the sensory pond and the valley bottom, and 530 fruit and nut trees in a designated woodland zone beside the path. Two very special trees, a magnolia and a 16-foot-high red horse chestnut, were also planted in the sensory gardens in memory of Jane.

In the workshops, a new manager, Mike Betts, embarked on an ambitious scheme to build two bird-watching hides for the valley and a set of raised wooden walk-ways which would make them accessible to wheelchairs. Alan, who had been involved in the workshops for many years, assured Mike that *he* would be able to train *him*, but Mike soon had a very happy and effective production line running. Because it involved using the most dangerous machinery, he would do the cutting out himself, then Alan would assemble or screw the items together. Antony, who preferred not to stand while he was working, was given the task of sanding down (and was once to be found, intent upon the job, completely inside the piece of furniture he was working on). All the items produced, including bird feeders, tables and plant troughs could be used round the farm as well as sold at Open Days. They were collected together to await the arrival of a very disturbed young man who came to the project every Thursday afternoon. He had found his niche in the workshop and loved painting on the wood stain. Finally, a lad who was new to the project and very nervous, took great pride in his allocated responsibility of fixing the Caring For Life tags on all the finished items.

With the access restrictions lifted, it was now possible to market the day-care products to visitors. The first Open Day since the Harvest Thanksgiving of 2000 was held in April 2002, just as the daffodils planted out over the winter came into bloom. This was followed by a plant sales day in May and the annual Open Day in June. The plant sales day was a great success, achieving record sales in plants, meat and eggs, despite atrocious weather. David, from Tindall House, who had prayed for sunshine, was not in the least put out by the wind and rain, assuring everyone in his own unique and inimitable style that the next Open Day would be fine. When asked why, he replied, 'Well! I prayed for good weather for the Open Day, but I meant for this plant sales day, but Jesus must have thought that I meant the June Open Day, so it will be good weather at the next one!'

His child-like faith was rewarded for, despite a gloomy

forecast, the day remained fine and was even graced, unintentionally, by a salute from the Red Arrows. The most remarkable outcome, however, was the amount of money raised. Instead of merely covering its costs, as had been expected, the Open Day produced the amazing sum of £14,000 through sales and donations on the day itself. That this day was such a triumph was particularly poignant and emotional for Peter, for it was the last time that he served in his capacity as chairman of the trustees. The same weekend both he and Judith resigned their trusteeships of Caring For Life.

The reason for this dramatic move was that Peter's health had been declining for many years. His personal legacy from the involvement in Romania was irreparable damage to his kidneys. Various spells in hospital had not been able to improve matters and in November 2001 he had had an operation in preparation for dialysis three times a week. The strain of working full-time as pastor of Leeds Reformed Baptist Church and chairman of the trustees of Caring For Life was simply more than he could manage. He had therefore reluctantly decided that he would have to retire as pastor of the church he had founded 30 years earlier and resign his post at Caring For Life. His long-time friend and colleague, David Kingdon, became the new chairman of trustees in his stead, and two much younger trustees, Neil Deacon, who had been the charity's first TFJ, and Mark Milsom, a senior police officer, were appointed to the board. A great deal of the day-to-day management had already devolved upon younger members of the team, including Peter's sons, Jonathan and Tim, with Florence Hendriksz, who managed the financial side of things. Steve Hoey, a former TFJ, had taken over the management of the resettlement team and Debbie Habib-zadeh the management of the horticulture, art and crafts and day-care. Together with one of the longest serving members, Judith Parkinson, they had all taken on a growing burden of responsibility as Peter was increasingly unable to fulfil his duties.

Despite taking these steps to ease Peter's workload, dialysis could not be a permanent solution to his deteriorating health and a kidney transplant offered the only hope. There was no suitable family donor and an existing heart condition meant that he was unlikely ever to be an appropriate recipient for an unrelated kidney from the small supply of post-humous donors. And then there was a miracle. Esther Smith had insisted that she, too, be tested for compatibility. Twelve months of testing finally produced the result for which no one had dared hope: it would be possible for her to donate a kidney. Esther's decision to make such an extraordinary personal sacrifice was typical; beneath a quiet and self-effacing exterior, she hid a heart that was generous to a fault and a spirit that was firmly anchored on Christ. She could also be formidably tenacious and determined, as many officious bureaucrats standing in the way of the welfare of Caring For Life's young people discovered to their cost. Unable to dissuade her from making the donation, Peter, his family and friends had to accept it in the same spirit that it was given. Although they were assured that removing a kidney would not endanger Esther's own health, there were inevitable risks to such a major operation, and it would necessitate a long period of recuperation which would see the two most important figures at Caring For Life out of action for many months.

The Christmas period was therefore one of more than usual uncertainty as the transplant operation, originally scheduled for 10 January 2003, was deferred by the hospital until the 31st. At the annual Christmas Eve party, there was a particularly emotional moment when Danny – not one of the most articulate residents of Tindall House – stood up and sang a song he had written for Peter and Esther. Written to the tune of Robbie Williams's hit 'Angels', it included the lines:

Esther and Pete, a dozen angels watching over you
And do you know we're praying every day that all goes well
Yes, Esther and Peter, your love shines through in all the things you do
So when I'm praying with my friends God's listening to us all
And answering our prayer;
God is so good to us all

The operation finally went ahead on 31 January 2003 and was initially a great success. Esther made steady progress, although she was extremely tired, and the doctors said that they had never seen a kidney from an unrelated donor perform as well as Esther's did in Peter. However, on 24 February, Peter had to return to hospital, having suffered a heart attack as a consequence of the operation. This was a major setback, but he recovered and by the summer he was well enough to attend the Open Day in June and even to consider taking up an active role again.

What was most encouraging, however, was the fact that Caring For Life had continued to function without its two principals. Tindall House underwent a major refurbishment which was completed a week ahead of schedule. And the long-delayed work on building an extension to Wendy Margaret Home to house five new girls was at last under way. This had been shelved many times simply because funding was not available, but now it had become an absolute necessity. New government legislation was coming into force which abolished the national system of funding for the care element of housing benefit and replaced it with Supporting People funding administered by the local authority. Caring For Life had always received housing benefit for those living in its two homes, but unless Wendy Margaret Home had eight residents by 31 March 2003 then the charity would never be able to claim for more than the three girls currently living there. Almost more difficult than completing the work on time was choosing the girls who would become the new residents. This was a judgement of Solomon, for, however unpalatable it was to have to make choices in the face of desperate need, need alone could not determine the choice: it was essential that the new girls were capable of fitting in with the other residents and did not disrupt the family atmosphere that Caring For Life had striven to maintain; and, as at Tindall House, every potential new resident had to meet with the approval of those already living there.

Sophie Greeves, one of the pastoral support workers in the home, remembers going to collect a new resident from her tower block flat in inner-city Leeds, which the girl was afraid to leave for fear of being attacked by her former friends. The whole place was run down and neglected: the communal stairway stank and the girl's flat was filthy, with paint peeling off the walls, floorboards exposed, and furniture that was falling to pieces. The girl herself had long neglected her own personal hygiene and appearance, and a lot of work would be needed to help her regain her dignity. And yet she could not stop smiling: she knew that she had a way out and was going to a home where she could be loved and belong. Her transformation in the weeks that followed had to be seen to be believed.

Less dramatic transformations occurred on a daily basis. One evening as Sophie was busy in the kitchen, Christine came in and announced that she had bought a fish for Kelly, another of the residents. Since she rarely spent anything on anyone else, this act of generosity was surprising in itself. The girls all loved fish and chips and Sophie had been trying hard to dissuade them from eating them so often, because most of them were struggling with diets of one kind or another, but this was the sort of gesture that needed encouraging. She therefore brightly answered, 'That's very kind. I'm sure she'll enjoy eating it', only to discover that the fish was alive and well and swimming in a plastic bag. Though the incident made everyone laugh, it was also a touching demonstration of the way that the girls in the house could, and did, learn genuinely to care for one another.

Progress was also made on the farm. Despite the absence of the new Agricultural Project support worker, who had broken his wrist, Jonathan and Tim Watts, a TFJ, managed to dig 600 metres of trenches and lay drainage pipes in them to protect the paths in the conservation project, just in time to meet the funding deadline. The workshops had built a second bird-watching hide and installed it overlooking the sensory pond. Perhaps more significantly, this project had enabled two of the men to make huge personal progress. Both were very poorly and struggled with feelings of insecurity and isolation. One of them travelled from Bradford and getting in on time had always been a problem, particularly when he was unhappy. As his confidence had improved, so had his time-keeping, and now, for several months, he had been arriving well before nine o'clock in the morning. The other young man was so nervous that he had struggled to manage even an hour a week at the farm; now he looked forward to coming and was working an afternoon a week. A small step for most people, but a mountain for him to climb.

The resettlement team had also made enormous advances, thanks to the employment of three additional members of staff. They were now responsible for caring for 125 people in the community, ranging in age from 16 to 92. The plight of the elderly was movingly described in the August bulletin of 2003:

You are living in a one-bedroomed flat in a high-rise block. Your flat is reasonably comfortable but it has become your prison. The lifts are often broken, and you are scared to use them anyway. You still remember the day you were mugged in the lift and that week's money was taken, leaving you with a badly bruised eye and a dread of going out.

Going down the steps can be frightening because of the gangs that hang around, and you prefer to stay in, never going out until it is absolutely necessary. Even the flat caretaker frightens you.

No one remembers your birthday. Christmas means nothing, and no one cares anyway.

An example of another, unfortunately typical, referral was a woman living on a large council estate in Leeds who had major problems with debt. When a member of the resettlement team rang her to arrange an appointment, she asked for a visit as soon as possible. Thirty minutes later she was found sitting in her lounge with a bottle of whisky and a row of tablets lined up on the table, ready to take her own life. She had not expected such a prompt response because she had been let down so many times before, but with Caring For Life's support she was able to re-schedule her debts and begin to regain control of her life.

In the midst of such tragedies, there were occasional glimpses of grim humour. Steve Hoey attended a case conference with one girl at which her social worker's repeated corrections to her comments finally drove her to cry, 'If you say that to me one more time I am going to go and commit suicide again!' On another occasion, a young man who was almost always very rude demanded, 'Steve, take me to town!' With the exemplary patience for which he is well known,

Steve replied, 'What's the magic word?' to which he received the abrupt response 'NOW!'

The Open Day of 2003 was, more than usually, a celebration for Caring For Life and its supporters. Both Peter and Esther were able to be present, to the great joy of all the young people, and there was one especially moving testament to the love that they had inspired. Danny managed to cap the emotional impact of his Christmas song by presenting Esther with a glass vase inscribed on its base 'Esther Smith, a woman of courage with a heart of gold'. Presenting it to her publicly, he moved his audience to tears: 'If it hadn't been for Esther's tremendous courage and faith, Peter's life would have been cut short,' he told them. 'Esther and Peter are very special people to everyone here at Caring For Life.'

A public expression of gratitude was also due to the charity's many supporters. The day before the auditors had expressed amazement at the miraculous way the sacrificial giving of individual supporters had offset the huge losses sustained from declining charitable trust income. (A falling stock market had obliged many grant-making bodies to cut back their support, resulting in the loss of £63,000 over three years from one fund alone.) Yet despite the reduced funding from charitable trusts, and the fact that the new Supporting People initiative did not issue any of the due payments correctly or in full for six months, Caring For Life was still able to meet its obligations. More than 58% of the charity's income was now drawn from its Christian support basis.

It was becoming ever clearer that this was going to be the

A Time of Miracles

only reliable source of funding in future. Grant-making trusts were becoming wary of falling foul of increasingly stringent anti-discrimination legislation. As a Christian charity, Caring For Life had always exercised a policy of employing only committed Christians as full-time staff. The Trust Deed of the charity also specifically stated that its objective was the promotion of the evangelical Christian faith through the provision of homes for the vulnerable. This did not mean that all those coming to Caring For Life were to be subjected to aggressive evangelization and expected to convert to Christianity. As the training programme for all staff and volunteers makes explicitly clear, to do so would be a terrible abuse of trust. The young people (and indeed those of all ages) who come to Caring For Life are extraordinarily vulnerable. In the past they have been betrayed by those closest to them – their families – the very people who should have done most to protect them. Teaching them to trust again, by becoming part of the wider Caring For Life family, lays them open to abuse once more. What most of them want, more than anything else, is to be accepted and loved. If they think that they can gain acceptance and love merely by going to church and professing to be Christian, then their hopes are going to be cruelly deceived. Saying prayers in parrot-fashion will not earn them a place in heaven; only a fundamental change of heart that will bring them to the love of God through Jesus Christ. For this reason, everyone working at Caring For Life is warned that they should never ask if someone wants to be a Christian and should only share their Christian views when appropriate or if invited to do so. There is a world of difference between this attitude and that of some other so-called 'fundamentalist evangelical Christians', whose extremism and fanaticism discredits all Christian ministries by its manipulation of vulnerable people into what is effectively cult membership. Sharing the love of Jesus lies at the heart of Caring For Life, but it is a passive rather than an active ministry. Though coming to faith in Christ Jesus is what Caring For Life would wish for all in its care, this is not to be achieved by indoctrination or pressure, but rather, as Christ himself had demonstrated, by loving example. And however much those working for the charity might long to see the men and women in their care come to faith, their love for these suffering people, like Christ's, has to be unconditional. 'It can take many months, even years, of watching and listening before someone will want to hear the good news of the gospel,' Esther would write in 2004. 'But from "square one" they see Christ's love in action and they take note of to Whom we belong.'

The gathering cloud on the horizon was even more threatening. The change from nationally administered housing benefit to locally managed Supporting People funding had taken place, ironically (but appropriately), on 1 April 2003. On paper at least, the new system could have been designed for Caring For Life because it envisaged exactly the sort of work the charity did in helping vulnerable people to maintain tenancies and live independently, providing them with a range of services and activities tailored to an individual's specific need, including 'a home visit for a short period each week or an on-site full-time support worker for a long period of time'.[26] In order to access the funds, Caring For Life had to submit costings to run the services and sign an intermediate contract with the local authority. Some implications of the contract, as we shall see, were completely unacceptable to the charity. More insidious problems were that the funding would only be guaranteed for a limited period, when the situation would be reviewed, and that there would be no automatic right to Supporting People money for those living in any new homes that might be opened. Since 124 requests had been received for places at Tindall House in 2002 alone – and none had been available – the need for such homes was demonstrably acute, but most local authorities preferred the cheaper option of supporting people in their own homes. And as would soon become clear, the issue of providing support beyond the short term, which was defined as two years, would become hugely contentious.

It was much easier to respond to such pressures by changing employment policies and understating or glossing over the Christian ethos simply in order to attract funds. And given the need for the work, and its unrivalled quality, few would have blamed Caring For Life if it had chosen to go down this route – as many other Christian charities did. Yet Peter and Esther were determined that they could not compromise their principles:

> Many people have worried at the risks we have taken
> – sometimes concerned by our forging ahead into

---

26 *What Is Supporting People?* Office of the Deputy Prime Minister Information Leaflet, 12 July 2004: www.spkweb.org.uk.

uncertainty where greater caution would be the route chosen by the most prudent. My own passionate belief is this – we have just one opportunity to pass this way. Faith demands, the gospel requires, that we must seize the day and go forward in faith. The retreating army seldom wins the day . . . Our growth has never been determined by our ability to cope, but by the needs which the Lord presents to us. If there really is a need we MUST find a way to address it . . . We can do all things through Christ who gives us strength.

The battle for Supporting People funding had only just been joined, but it would continue to cast its shadow for years to come. Caring For Life's survival, and certainly its expansion in future, would have to depend increasingly on the support of its Christian prayer partners.

9

Supporting People

One Friday evening in late February 2004, just as a group of the young people who had stayed on at the farm for Bible study were preparing to go home, they noticed what they thought was a bonfire on neighbouring land. Then a distressed lady ran up the lane – still wearing her slippers – and begged for help. Vandals had set fire to the hay in her barn: she had managed to rescue the horses in the adjoining stable, but the fire service needed assistance in removing the blazing bales from the barn to prevent the fire spreading. Peter and Danny, from Tindall House, immediately set off on the tractor and, with the help of Chris Wilson, who joined them later, they worked into the early hours of the morning to drag the burning bales outside and spread them out so that they could be dampened down with fire hoses. Though the barn was destroyed by the fire, the stable block was saved and, in the process, Caring For Life had won another friend.

A few weeks later, on 14 April, one of the charity's oldest and most dedicated supporters died. Peter's 94-year-old mother, 'Aunty Lily', had been a key figure in helping the charity to get off the ground, financing the setting up of the original day-care schemes, acting as a scrupulously careful and accurate book-keeper (despite using neither a calculator nor a computer), and offering practical assistance round the farm. Even when she became less able, she remained a watchful presence, reporting those whom she had seen from her bedroom window who appeared to be slacking in their work or taking early tea-breaks. She insisted on being introduced to every newcomer to the charity and she was much loved by all the young people who enjoyed having 'special chats' with her. Her death left a considerable void but it was some comfort that she died, as she had lived, in faith, and passed peacefully into glory in the presence of those who loved her.

'Aunty Lily' died just before one of the most exciting days in Caring For Life's history. On 19 May, HRH The Countess of Wessex paid an official visit to the farm. Partly in preparation for her visit, but principally in order to comply with new Health and Safety regulations, both the Resource Centre and the workshop had undergone a major overhaul. The Resource Centre needed a separate food storage area (which would also create space for the improvement of the kitchen) and a new shower and toilet block which would include separate disabled access for both men and women. In order to do the necessary work, Caring For Life had contacted CRASH, a construction and property industry charity, which offer the expertise of its patron companies to assist charities and agencies dealing with the homeless to improve their premises and enable them to deliver better services to their clients. CRASH put Caring For Life in touch with Wates Group and, after a visit to Crag House Farm, the staff of the local Leeds office took up the project with enthusiasm. They persuaded a local architect to produce the plans and carried out the work at a price which was described as 'extremely charitable'. CRASH sourced some of the building materials required at a reduced rate and, in some cases, completely free of charge; exceptionally, it also made a donation of £35,000 towards the cost of this project. Just as valuable in the longer term was the fact that the introduction to Wates proved to be the start of an enduring relationship. Seeing at first hand the value and practical success of Caring For Life's work, the company adopted it as its charity of the year and began a major programme of fund-raising which would continue well into the future.[27]

Generous grants were also responsible for the installation of new machinery in the workshops which was required to meet the higher standards of the new safety legislation. One of those grants, which had enabled the purchase of a band saw, had come from the Earl and Countess of Wessex Charitable Trust (now renamed the Wessex Youth Trust) and it was partly in order to see this in place that the Countess had agreed to visit the farm. For staff, volunteers and especially the young people, the day of her visit was the culmination of weeks of hard work, so it was a tremendous thrill for them to see how genuinely moved and interested she was in everything she saw. She toured the entire farm, from sensory gardens to the poly-tunnels, meat and egg preparation

---

27 Most recently, Wates have offered generous assistance in building the new Adult Learning Centre.

rooms to stables and workshops. More importantly, she engaged sympathetically with all the young people, making a special effort to talk to everyone. To this day, Alan remains inordinately proud of the fact that the Countess accepted a hand-carved walking-stick that he had made specially for her and tells everyone, as she had told him, that she would use it while walking in Scotland.

Gary was equally proud of the encouragement that she had given him. Two years earlier, he had embarked on a new day-care project, a literacy and numeracy programme, which had been set up by Michael Coles during his year of office as president of the Headingley Rotary Club. Staffed by members of the club, together with volunteers such as Collette Crossen, a retired special needs teacher, the scheme had enabled one-to-one tuition to take place on a weekly basis. Illiteracy and innumeracy are huge problems, making people who are already vulnerable even more so, especially once they reach adulthood and are ashamed to admit that they cannot tell the time, write a letter, recognize bus numbers or count their money in a shop. Now Gary, who would go on to write his own life story with the assistance of his tutors on the scheme, was able to demonstrate his new-found skills to the Countess and write afterwards:

The royal visit was amazing. When she came over to me, she ... Looking [*sic*] at my spelling and sums. She asked me to do a sum for her and I got it right – I didn't use a calculator, just my head. She really liked the Letter I gave her – she said at [*sic*] was really neat.

The Countess even won universal approval from the more critical girls of Wendy Margaret Home who admired her face, her hair, and her elegant cream trouser suit, as well as her kindness to them. 'I thought she was very nice and pretty,' wrote Catherine, who had met her in the sensory gardens, 'and I liked it at the end when she was telling me that she likes gardening but she can't do too much of it because of her baby.' For everyone there the highlight of the day was when the Countess came to say goodbye. Having greatly over-stayed her allotted time, instead of simply disappearing with a regal wave, she insisted on gathering all the young people together, plunged into their midst and, with her arms around them, posed for a group photograph. It was an indication of how much the visit had also meant to her that, a year later, the Countess agreed to become the charity's patron, insisting that she did not intend this to be merely an honorary role but an active one. She was as good as her word. The Wessex Youth Trust paid for a new vacuum-packing machine for the meat preparation room and a new oven and grill for the Resource Centre kitchen. And in October 2006 she would return again to pay another visit to the farm and to host the charity's first fund-raising banquet.

One of the unintended consequences of the Countess's visit was that it introduced many of those who accompanied her that day to the work of Caring For Life. As was custom-ary on royal visits, the Lord Lieutenant of West Yorkshire, Dr Ingrid Roscoe, and the High Sheriff of the county, Mr James Barker, were in attendance. Both were new to their posts and taking part in their first royal visit, so it would always have been a memorable day. What made it so special was witnessing the difference that Caring For Life had made to the lives of those who had previously known nothing but the pain of abuse, ostracism and rejection. Crag House Farm should have been a place of silence and misery; instead it was full of life and laughter and love. Not just the staff and volunteers, but also many of the young people themselves were eager to share with these visitors the love of Jesus which had changed their own lives beyond all recognition. It was a truly humbling experience. And it made both the Lord Lieutenant and the High Sheriff determined to do all they could in the future to help the unsung but quite wonderful ministry of Caring For Life.

The charity was in need of champions, for the euphoria of the Countess's visit was followed by catastrophic news. In the summer of 2004 the charity learnt that the local authority assessors sent to review Caring For Life's services and approve them for Supporting People funding had given them what was in effect a 'failed' scoring on every single count. The likely consequence would be a total withdrawal of the funding, amounting to a loss of over £270,000 the following year. The decision was completely incomprehensible to anyone who had experienced even a fraction of the charity's work. Even if one only looked at the quantity, rather than the quality (though the latter obviously determined the former), the figures spoke for themselves. Caring For Life's record was nationally unrivalled: 97% of those re-housed by the charity did not become homeless again; 85% of those with criminal records did not re-offend.

'We recognize that we are far from perfect,' Peter wrote in the July 2004 bulletin:

> But we also are aware that we have taken the greatest care to honour the Lord in the way in which we undertake our ministry and care for our people. There is an authority to whom we are accountable, infinitely more important than either a local authority or national government, and that is the Lord of Lords. He visits and inspects us daily, and we are deeply conscious of that. Therefore we have sought to conduct ALL our affairs in a way that pleases Him and meets with His standards. We are confident that the service we provide is of the highest standard, particularly in terms of the protection and the quality of compassionate, loving Christian care that we offer.

This, however, was the problem. The process and framework of the assessment were new and the assessors inexperienced in using them, but it was readily apparent from the comments in their report that the Christian essence at the core of Caring For Life's work had caused some antagonism. They had broken the government's guidelines by taking 19 weeks to issue their report, but the assessment had not been carried out robustly, and evidence that contradicted their conclusions had been omitted – even though it had been brought to their attention at the time. Worse still, many of the young people in residential care had been deeply upset by being interviewed in the absence of the staff who cared for them on a daily basis, and by being required to fill in a questionnaire which asked intimate personal details about, for instance, their sexuality, which were deeply inappropriate for vulnerable victims of sexual abuse.

'We will and have recognized where our ministry and our services could be improved and have sought to respond immediately to any justified criticism,' Peter informed supporters, 'but we will be resolute in not being willing under any circumstances to compromise our Christian convictions.' As if to underscore the meaning and purpose of Caring For Life's ministry, one of the first people the charity had cared for returned to its orbit seeking help. Peter describes her story, which had helped to inspire the foundation of Caring For Life:

My first realization of the horrors of violence and sexual abuse that some children can endure came when I met a little 13-year-old girl. She was in Esther's care in a small group children's home more than 20 years ago. Although her mother's partner had frequently raped her since she was 10 years of age, and in spite of Esther's pleas and protests, social services made the child return home to the mother and the abusive partner every weekend. Every Sunday night she returned to Esther with stories of rape, abuse and unspeakably evil things that she had been forced to do. Many times her plight brought us to tears. I would move from the deepest distress for the child to the most intense anger against the man who abused her, and also toward those who so blindly sent her back again and again into the cauldron of suffering. Not until she was 18 could we help her. But systematic abuse from the age of ten leaves terrible scars. So often such victims stumble along paths of self-destruction, stability and happiness eluding them.

But today our little 13-year-old came home again, seeking the love of a family who won't hurt her and who is always there . . . She is now 34 years old, cared for by our resettlement team, and plans to come to the farm for day care. Before she left, she asked how to get to our Sunday services; she wants to come back to church again.

That is what we at Caring For Life are about. We are there, always there, for those who have never heard of us before and for those who are 'coming back home' to where they know they will find love, compassion, safety and – most of all – Jesus!

The daily stress of being constantly available to such desperately needy people was exacerbated by the uphill battle to retain Supporting People funding and it took its toll. Esther, on whom the principal burden of extra administration fell, was exhausted and Peter, trying as always to do too much, ruptured his transplant scar, necessitating another operation. The offer of a meeting to review the omitted evidence was first held out by the assessors and then withdrawn. Informal discussions raised issues that were resolved, only for new issues to arise. Requiring all those who lived in either of the two homes to attend the day-care schemes at the farm throughout the week, unless they were in employment, attended college or had other scheduled activities, was condemned outright, even though it was widely recognized that this was a major factor in the charity's success. The fact that the young people enjoyed the activities and benefited hugely from them was irrelevant: if they wished to stay at home and do nothing all day, then that, the assessors argued, was their inalienable right.

Another crucial sticking point was the charity's commitment to lifelong care, especially for those in its residential homes. The general thinking with regard to working with homeless people, or those at risk of homelessness, is currently that this should be for a maximum of two years, by which time they should have achieved independence. As those at Caring For Life knew all too well, tackling the problem of homelessness is not just about finding accommodation, but about addressing its root causes – learning difficulties, mental illness, low self-esteem, addiction, criminal convictions and lack of family support. Addressing these issues may take years, even a lifetime, and although it was possible that some of the residents of Tindall House or Wendy Margaret Home might eventually graduate to living in their own accommodation, providing that they had continuing support, for the majority this would never be an option. And to cancel support for such damaged and vulnerable people – or worse still eject them from the security of their homes after two years – simply because an arbitrary time limit had been reached would not only be cruel but also disastrous. This Caring For Life refused to do. The promise was to be there for as long as was wanted or needed, regardless of the financial consequences.

News that another local organization providing a long-term supported home for those with multiple needs would now have to close because its Supporting People funds were being withdrawn was a further blow to Caring For Life's own hopes. As Peter was hospitalized for the second time in the year since he had become chief executive, the temptation to give up the unequal battle was strong. Only an unfaltering conviction that the Lord had never failed them before, and a sense that they had a sacred duty to perform, kept the team going through these difficult times. And despite an uncertain future, everywhere there was evidence of God's grace and blessing. The Open Days and sales days welcomed more people than ever before to the farm, and the stand at the Great Yorkshire Show was overwhelmed by a continuous stream of supporters calling in to express their approval of the charity's uncompromisingly Christian stance. Its Christian ministry won the support of the Anglican bishops of Ripon and Leeds and of Wakefield, the latter of whom hosted a highly successful garden party for supporters in the grounds of his house. The charity's unrivalled record in preventing re-offending won the admiration and approval of the High Court judges on circuit in the county, leading them to sponsor a major fund-raising event on the charity's behalf at the Judges' Lodgings in Leeds. And on 2 June 2005, the anniversary of the Queen's coronation, acknowledging the vital role of faithful volunteers who did everything from planting hedgerows to cooking meals and teaching literacy and numeracy, it was announced that Caring For Life had been given the Queen's 'Unsung Heroes' Award for Voluntary Service. Praising this achievement, Paul Goggins, Minister for the Voluntary and Community Sector, declared, 'Groups like Caring For Life are a vital resource who make a difference to the everyday lives of so many people.' Everyone, it seemed, apart from the assessors of Supporting People, could see that the charity performed an outstanding service to the community.

With the threat of losing the funding hanging over both the residential homes and, potentially, also the resettlement project (now renamed 'Floating Support' to reflect its role in helping to maintain tenancies), the ladies working in the Public Relations team became ever more ingenious in their efforts to raise money. Set up in the aftermath of the withdrawal from Romania, they had long since demonstrated their worth by targeting grant-making bodies for the various projects at the farm and by travelling the country to make presentations to potential supporters in churches and Christian groups. The value of these 'partner churches' was immense. They offered not only spiritual support but also practical assistance. In 2004 alone, 98 churches sent harvest food and a further 43 raised more than £15,000 in harvest offerings. These donations enabled Caring For Life to serve 5,200 breakfasts and 7,800 lunches at the farm and to distribute 150 emergency food parcels and a further 100 Christmas hampers to those living in the community. (For Health and Safety reasons, every item donated has to be sorted and stored according to its expiry date. On one occasion, Danny from Tindall House was enthusiastically helping the TFJs to check the dates on tins – and was observed throwing every single tin of Heinz baked beans on to the 'out of date' pile. When he was asked why, he showed them the legend on the can, 'Heinz Established 1869'.)

The Computing and Media Project team, which produced all the posters, leaflets and bulletins for presentations, as well as the monthly news bulletin for supporters, introduced a catalogue of all the farm products available for sale in the small on-site shop, including beef, lamb, eggs, bird and bat boxes, walking sticks, bird tables, feeders and seed, plant troughs and wheelbarrow planters, as well as items made in the Arts and Crafts project, such as hand-made cards and small gifts. The products were also displayed on the website, www.caringforlife.co.uk, which had been brought in-house and was regularly updated by Tim Parkinson, with the help of David and Michael, both of whom had developed computer and office skills.

David and Michael were also involved in posting leaflets round the local estates to advertise the charity's products and its free-range egg delivery service. Martyn, who accompanied them, had given them simple and careful instructions: they were to go to the front door of each house, post the leaflet through the letterbox, and not get into long conversations with the people they might meet. David, who is autistic and therefore does exactly what he is asked to do, promptly marched up to one house, completely ignoring its owner who had seen him approaching and come to the door to receive the delivery. Without saying a word, David bent down, pushed the leaflet between the man's ankles and walked away. As Martyn struggled to offer an explanation and an apology, he turned round to check where Michael was, only to see that he had delivered a leaflet to the house next door and was now trying to negotiate a set of steps. Such was his phobia of steps that he was lying almost horizontal, hanging on to the railings and shuffling down virtually flat to the ground. Martyn decided to make his excuses and leave as quickly as possible, leaving the householder staring after them, totally dumb-founded.

The PR team had always encouraged sponsored events, such as an annual Christmas sleep-out overnight on the steps of Leeds City Hall by students and other supporters, which had regularly highlighted the problem of homelessness and raised the charity's profile. Now they redoubled their efforts. Adoption schemes were set up, enabling supporters to sponsor annually one of the gardens, ponds or animals, the horses and guinea pigs proving to be particular favourites. Supporters were urged to buy an extra book of stamps whenever they bought one for themselves and to send it to Caring For Life: a simple but effective idea, it raised £314.66 worth of stamps in its first month and almost £4,000 by the end of the year, which considerably reduced the charity's postage costs. For the more energetic there was a variety of sponsored walks with a twist (a 5-mile walk round five farms in the Cookridge area, balancing a fresh Crag House Farm egg on a spoon), tandem parachute jumps and a coast-to-coast bicycle ride. At the annual Open Day, in front of a thousand visitors and in blazing sunshine, Rod Wark, who had supported Caring For Life since its inception, completed a sponsored marathon on a rowing machine in just 2 hours 56 minutes, raising much-needed funds for refurbishments at Tindall House. Twelve months of intensive activity raised more than £21,000. A bid to draw more churches into Caring For Life's ambit was launched in the autumn of 2005 with 'Relaying the News', passing a baton from John O'Groats to Land's End by way of as many churches as possible.

An appeal also went out for new volunteers, whose role would be increasingly vital if Supporting Funding were withdrawn and as the number of referrals requiring one-on-one support increased. The contribution made by current volunteers was already indispensable: 'Put in the clearest terms, we could not sustain our present levels of support and ministry, nor sustain projects such as Conservation, Horticulture, Adult Literacy and Numeracy Training and even our Art and Craft projects, if it were not for some very faithful volunteers.' The problem, as with finding new staff, was to get people of the right calibre. The lives of those cared for are very fragile and some of them live every day on the edge. It can take just one telephone call or one letter from an unsympathetic parent or sibling to drive the recipient to self-harm or even suicide. Months of love and work can be undermined in seconds, and then the process has to be begun again from the beginning. There are so many vulnerable people looked after by Caring For Life that this happens on a weekly basis and it can, quite literally, be soul-destroying. Steve Hoey, the manager of the Floating Support team, summed up the challenge:

When I explain to people what my work involves, they often say, 'That must be very satisfying.' People also ask me if I enjoy my work. Most of the time we are dealing with very difficult issues, seeing young people hurting themselves and hearing tragic stories of abuse. This work is not often satisfying, or enjoyable! We are in this work because we feel that it is the right thing to do, and that the Lord himself has called us to do it.

The law requires that anyone working with vulnerable people has to be interviewed, vetted and cleared by the Criminal Records Bureau. Caring For Life demands a much higher standard: their volunteers would have to receive clearance from Christ. As an acknowledgement of their importance, in future all volunteers would be invited to join staff meetings, training days and retreats, thereby integrating them as fully as possible with the professional team. Whether it was half a day a week, a day a month, or a period of several weeks in the year, every contribution would be valuable, relieving the pressure on the staff but also enabling more people to be cared for by the charity.

The record crowds that flocked to the various Open Days at the farm and to the stand at the Great Yorkshire Show were a tangible demonstration of the level of grassroots support that the work of Caring For Life enjoyed. For the young people there was enormous pride in seeing their hard work rewarded when 'my' flowers were sold or 'my' produce was enjoyed at lunch. Even weeding, a task quite properly loathed by everyone, had its defenders. Sarah, a talented florist with deep psychological problems, remarked that clearing the soil reminded her of sins removed by Jesus. Her wonderful arrangements, often made with flowers, plants and seeds collected on the farm, were extremely popular with purchasers on Open Days, but had also won her second prize at the

Great Yorkshire Show in 2003. Her most moving creation, however, was the simple display that she did for the Caring For Life stand in 2005. It was an eloquent metaphor not only for her own plight but also that of most of those for whom the charity cared. It was a baby's cot with thistles, thorns and teasels growing out of it.

Many of those who had been cared for over the years had shown a desire to 'give something back' and one of the most remarkable examples occurred one summer. Jason was a Christian who had been supported by Caring For Life for over 14 years. Rejected by his mother at birth, he had endured a wretched childhood of violence and sexual abuse in numerous foster homes, and grew up to be a deeply disturbed man, distrustful, angry and full of hatred. He became alcoholic and suicidal. Dragged down into a spiralling vortex of spells in hostels, psychiatric hospitals and prison, he had ended up sleeping rough. (On one occasion, sleeping in a bus shelter, he had heard a group of lads say '"Let's get some petrol and set him on fire." But Jesus was with me and he looked after me.') Statutory bodies had washed their hands of him, saying that they could not find him a place, and no other agency would house him because of his violent and unpredictable behaviour.

As a last resort, and to save him from sleeping rough again, Caring For Life had housed him in a flat, but within four days he was suicidal, sniffing gas and begging to be sectioned. After another period in a psychiatric hospital, and only a week after being baptized, he tried to hang himself. Not long afterwards, while still trying, and failing, to get the psychiatric help he so desperately needed, he wrenched out his gas fire and, standing in the middle of his bed-sit with a box of matches, threatened to blow himself up. The police were forced to evacuate eight neighbouring streets in the middle of the night and, as a result, Jason received a prison sentence. In his absence, his wife, with whom he had a stormy relationship and whose past was as troubled as his own, gave birth to their daughter who was immediately taken into care.

Released in time for the 2003 Open Day, he had offered up a sincere prayer of gratitude for his freedom, for his daughter being placed in a good home, and for 'bringing me home to my family here at Caring For Life'. Then this grown man, almost 40 years old, added, 'I thank you for my family at Caring For Life. That here I can have a dad and brothers and sisters, and uncles and aunties who really love me, and who love everybody that comes here.' Thereafter, Peter's sons had to grow used to hearing their father referred to as 'our Dad' and Judith was surprised and delighted to receive a Mother's Day card from her new 'son'. A couple of years later, when Jason had become a stalwart on the farm, taking especial pleasure in looking after the longhorn cattle, he was called out to find a calf that had been dropped some way from the herd and abandoned by its mother. Jason decided to hand-rear the calf and showed remarkable devotion and tenderness in caring for it, but it was his prayer on its behalf that moved those listening to tears: 'Dear heavenly father, I pray for the calf whose mother has deserted him. I do pray that one day she will come to him and accept him, that one day he will meet with his mother, that she will love him.' Unable to articulate his emotions at his own rejection at birth, he had finally found the words, but selflessly for another being.

Now, in the summer of 2005, Jason decided that he would undertake a sponsored run on behalf of Caring For Life. What is more, this was no ordinary run but 20 miles up- and downhill from Skipton, on the edge of the Yorkshire Dales, to Crag House Farm. No one expected that he would be able to complete such a distance, let alone on such an arduous course, but he was absolutely determined to do it and surprised everyone, maintaining a steady 8 miles an hour, and arriving, exhausted but triumphant, to a rapturous reception at the farm. He had raised more than £400 by this effort, but seeing the pride on his face was a greater reward for his 'family' at Caring For Life.

Jason's story – and his struggles continue to this day – was a powerful demonstration of the importance of offering life-long support. Another young man, 23 years old, had been referred to Caring For Life because the agency that looked after him had come to the end of the usual two-year period of care and, anxious not to lose its funding, needed to get him off their books. He struggled with reading, writing and budgeting and was in constant danger of losing his tenancy because he did not understand the importance of paying rent, bills and debts. Miraculously, he had avoided drugs, even though his brothers were dealers and he was under constant pressure to live up to their profligate lifestyle. Had the Floating Support team not taken him under their wing, with the promise that they would be there for as long as he needed them, there is little doubt that he would have lost his tenancy and become just another nameless faceless statistic in the homelessness tables. Instead, he not only coped well in his new house but also enrolled at college to progress his skills. George, who accompanied him to his interview at his request, also helped him fill in the application forms. The young man managed to fill in his name and address, but then got stuck. 'I always struggle with this one,' he told George. The question was 'Male or Female?'

As a direct result of the Supporting People review of costs and value for money, a number of hostels in Leeds were forced to close, including one for homeless young men and another for young women, which both shut in the summer of 2005. The hostel staff were under pressure to re-house these vulnerable people, but were deeply concerned that many of them would not be able to cope with independent living. The terrible irony was that one hostel therefore referred virtually every single one of their former residents to the Caring For Life Floating Support team – the only agency that could be trusted to look after them successfully – despite the fact that this self-same agency had, in effect, been failed and declared inadequate by the assessors of Supporting People. Eighty-three new referrals were received in the first nine months of the year, a workload that was utterly beyond the charity's capability.

One of those evicted as her supported home closed was Sue, who had been unspeakably abused and exploited in earlier life. Extremely damaged and very angry, she had been referred to the day-care schemes at Caring For Life ten years previously. Although she had at first been bitterly hostile to the Christian ethos, ten years of compassion, sympathy, support and unconditional love had softened her heart, but she remained a tragic and pathetic figure. One cold winter's evening Peter and Judith had returned from church to find her curled up in their porch at the farm because she had nowhere else to sleep that night. In the summer of 2005 she was the last remaining resident of her supported home which was about to close. She had applied for a place at Wendy Margaret Home, but none was available. Unable to contemplate the future, she had doused herself in petrol and attempted to set herself alight. As a result of this suicide attempt, she ought to have been admitted to hospital, but there were no beds available. Truly, there was no room at the inn for this unhappy woman. And a few weeks later she took an overdose and succeeded in killing herself: just one more victim of man's inhumanity to man, but one who had, at least belatedly in her short life, had the love of Jesus shared with her.

10

Twenty Years and Beyond

The new year, 2006, opened with a series of salutary lessons in the fragility and vulnerability of the people in the care of Caring For Life. In January alone, an ambulance had to be called on three separate occasions to the farm and twice to Wendy Margaret Home, and in one extreme emergency, when one of the ladies had a very serious epileptic fit, the air ambulance had to be called out. There were three visits to the Accident and Emergency department of the local hospital – including one that caused much wry laughter when the unfortunate lady, suffering another fit, complained that she was missing *Casualty* on the television.

There were also, as always, tragic stories of people who were beyond help. Keith had been a chronic alcoholic for 30 years; he had also continually self-harmed and had been admitted 84 times to the local hospital as a result. This had stopped when he met Sarah, but she too was an alcoholic whose sole aim in life was to remain in a drunken stupor to numb the pain of an unbearable past. Together they had tried to conquer their addictions in the hope of having Sarah's two children returned to her. They had been visited by the Floating Support team for the first time just before Christmas and had been invited to spend Christmas Day at the farm, but when a member of staff called to pick them up he was told that Sarah, whose condition was complicated by worsening epilepsy, was too ill to come. A Christmas dinner was taken round to their home, but no one answered the door. Several telephone calls to Keith resulted in a visit being arranged for 5 January, but the day before Sarah was found dead. A window had closed, a life lost, and a fragile broken heart had stopped for ever.

The same month also saw the return to prison of Antony. He had now lived at Tindall House for 18 years, and although he had changed immeasurably since he first came to Caring For Life, not least in becoming a committed Christian, he had never completely overcome his patterns of compulsive behaviour. The worst of these was his tendency, when feeling anxious, unhappy or threatened, to wander into other people's houses, sometimes stealing small items, sometimes simply standing there in silence. (Antony had hated camping in Wales on a Caring For Life trip and had walked into a house, sat in the middle of the lounge until the owners came in, refused to move and asked to be arrested. 'Prison would be better than living in tents,' he had then declared.) Although it was unclear on this occasion whether he had stolen anything, he had terrified the residents, who had found him silently standing in their house. Since he was in breach of a curfew order, he was fortunate to escape a much longer sentence, but his judge, after reading the reports from Caring For Life and noting their supportive presence in court, was

163

compassionate. Antony was given the minimum sentence possible, 12 months in prison, reduced to six months for good behaviour. He was equally fortunate in finding sympathetic officers at Armley Prison, who took account of his multiple disabilities, which now included diabetes, and ensured that he served his sentence in the comparative safety of the hospital wing of the prison. Some weeks later, in response to 1 of more than 200 letters and cards he had received in prison, he wrote:

> I am so fortunate and lucky to have such good friends and such good care and support from Caring For Life I do not deserve it when I do bad things and get into trouble I will never do it again I do not want to let my friends and Caring For Life down again and especially I do not want to let Deborah [a resident of Wendy Margaret Home to whom he had just become engaged] down. I thank God every day that I have so many very good friends and I thank Him for Caring For Life and for Deborah ... God is with me He has kept me safe here ... God bless and thanks for everything you have done for me.

The judge at Antony's trial had gone out of his way to commend the work and ministry of Caring For Life in the highest possible terms. A few weeks later, there was another accolade: the awarding of the Investors in People standard. The assessor, in his report, paid a glowing tribute to the ethos of the charity: 'I feel that it is a veritable strength of Caring For Life that people do feel recognized for their efforts. There is a care and concern for people, whether staff, volunteers or the young people themselves that I have not seen anywhere else.'

One of the many young TFJs who had given a year of their lives to the charity echoed this sentiment, but also explained why she had found the work rewarding:

I'm not sure what I expected life as a TFJ volunteer to be like, but the year so far has been an experience unlike any other! I started in September, wondering quite what I had let myself in for. Yet through working alongside the young people on projects such as horticulture, small mammals, helping Joe with the horses or working in the kitchen, being a TFJ at Caring For Life has taught me so much about myself, the vulnerable people we care for and how God wants me to serve Him now and in the future. I love that no two days are ever the same and that every day we are allowed the privilege of loving and caring for people in a real and practical way. The last six months have been happy and sad, heartbreaking but inspiring, educating, humbling, lots and lots of fun and I'm looking forward to what God has in store during the next six months!

The many talents of the staff were also being put to good use with the introduction of several important new day-care projects. A much expanded equestrian project was introduced on the death of Luther, the elderly shire-horse, who had been a much-loved asset of the farm almost since the charity's inception. With more horses, of varying breeds and sizes, and a new supervisor, Judith Whiteley, who was an experienced teacher of Riding for the Disabled, the potential for opening up the project to more people was enormous. And for Joe, who had been devoted to Luther, looking after and training the new horses for riding and driving was a lifeline.

In order to meet all the Health and Safety requirements of registered food premises, including proper storage, preparation and handling of food, Caring For Life had appointed its first full-time chef, Mark Newsome, a former volunteer who was also an experienced professional chef. Though his primary remit was to prepare breakfast and lunch each day, ensuring that all those attending the farm were provided with healthy, good-quality meals using the farm's own produce, he also set up a new Catering Academy for four students at a time. The course began with a month of twice-weekly afternoon sessions learning about food hygiene, nutrition, healthy living and Health and Safety standards. Only once the students had passed the relevant tests were they allowed into the kitchen where, for one day a week, they enjoyed individual training with Mark, preparing all the meals for those attending day-care. An enormous hit with the young people, who were soon practising their newly acquired culinary skills at home, the course was designed not only to give confidence but also to help those with problems of over-eating, under-eating, food phobias and intolerances.

At about the same time two new workshops, one in music and one in drama, were also introduced. These were of particular value to the many young people who suffered from speech impediments. (At times the Resource Centre can sound like a perfect Babel, with everyone chattering away nineteen to the dozen in their own highly individual style; the remarkable thing is that although those with 'normal' speech sometimes find it impossible to work out what they are saying, they can all understand each other perfectly.) The music workshop relied on individual and group sessions and encouraged the young people to experiment with different instruments and musical activities, including singing. The drama workshop, set up by Joanna Cooper, a former professional actress, was divided into two sessions, one for ladies and one for men, and involved games, exercises for movement and posture, breathing techniques (particularly useful for calming nervous or excitable students) and voice production. Though the aim was to build confidence, release tension and, above all, have fun, the results were dramatic and often unexpected. Maxine, a resident of Wendy Margaret Home, with mental health problems and a number of physical disabilities, whose normal speech was virtually unintelligible, proved not only to have a beautiful singing voice but also, astonishingly, to be capable of perfect diction when acting a role in character. And it is easy to understand the bewilderment of one supporter who, watching a video clip of some of the staff and young people performing a very energetic morris-dance at an Open Day review, was heard to ask 'Which one's the autistic one?'

'It is always a joy to see someone in our care participating in some activity and doing so with obvious excitement, enjoyment and even pride, who only days before had responded to the invitation to participate with their invariable "I can't",' Peter explained. All too often the familiar and usually rather grumpy response to such invitations – 'I can't' or 'I don't want to!' – turned out to mean 'I don't think that I am capable of doing it' or even 'I am afraid of trying and making myself yet again look like an idiot!' The sheer range of activities now on offer meant that the likelihood of discovering a hidden talent was even greater than before – but it was just as important to encourage those whose abilities remained known to God alone.

Many of the people Caring For Life tries to help manifest their problems by various forms of disruptive attention-seeking: being over-loud or withdrawn, moody or just walking away. They need constant reassurance that they are much loved and special, that they should not try to compare themselves with others, but realize that they are unique and very precious to the God who made them. The expert advice of Gayle Nixon, a Senior Specialist Educational Psychologist, was particularly valuable in this area. In the summer of 2006, she volunteered to undertake assessments of some of those in the charity's care, identifying their learning needs and how these might best be addressed. One of the young people was absolutely thrilled by his assessment and could not wait to tell everyone that he had achieved a 'five' in his reading skills. What he did not realize – and what demonstrated so clearly Gayle's own empathy and skill – was that she had assessed his reading ability as that of a five-year-old. A great admirer of Caring For Life's work, Gayle would become involved in training staff and volunteers, helping them to achieve even higher standards of care by increasing their understanding of the problems faced by those they supported.

Those problems were graphically illustrated by the work-load of the Floating Support team during a single week in July 2006. The week began with the death of one of the men they supported and ended with an arson attack on a house which left all the residents homeless, including two men they supported, one of whom was then attacked and raped. In between, another man they cared for was burgled and they discovered from the boyfriend of a 17-year-old girl who was due to have a baby in two weeks' time that the girl's father was a convicted child sex offender. For the protection of her unborn child, the team referred the case to Social Services and, attending a subsequent meeting between the couple and social workers, brokered an agreement that would allow the couple to keep their baby, providing that Caring For Life found them a new home and the abusive grandfather was not allowed any contact. They also found new homes for the two victims of the arsonist.

These were all people living out in the selfish, violent, amoral and brutal world laughably termed 'the community'. People like Jason who, after 15 years of support from Caring For Life, was now too afraid to return to his flat because he had been threatened by his neighbours. He turned up drunk and distressed at Crag House Farm, the only fixed place in his universe, and the only one where he had ever known affection. Unable to stay there, in his desperation he self-harmed himself so badly that he ended up in hospital again. These were the people whose lifelong problems government policy had decreed should be resolved within two years, on pain of withdrawal of supportive funding. In a 'quick-fix' age,

government strategy was being driven by financial consid-
erations and the desire to create the illusion that its policies
were successful. If a person had enjoyed two years of Supporting People funding and was then pushed out into the
world so that he could be taken off the books, statistically his
care was deemed to have been a success. And with the media
forever denouncing the 'idle' and the 'work-shy' who milked
the benefit system and lived off hand-outs from the taxpayer,
who could blame the government's response?

As Caring For Life had repeatedly and wearily stated so
many times over the years, there would always be those who
would never achieve complete independence and should
not be expected to do so, even if they lived 'in the community' rather than in a supported home like Tindall House or
Wendy Margaret Home. Yet, as the on-going battle to obtain
approval as a provider of services for Supporting People
funding demonstrated all too clearly, this need was not officially recognized – or funded. And there was no other agency
willing or able to pick up the cost of the care.

More than three years after the introduction of Supporting People, Caring For Life still had only an interim contract.
A much improved review decision had been received, after
tireless work by a new service development officer and one
of the trustees, and, as a result, the Commissioning Body
had at last sent a letter in October 2005 stating that it would
now commission the charity's services for both the Floating Support team and the two residential homes. The relief proved short-lived. On 22 June 2006, Peter and Esther
learnt that this decision was in jeopardy because the charity

had failed the accreditation process. Ironically, since the receipt of Supporting People funding made all the difference, the charity's financial position was considered untenable because it held no reserves. They were informed that funding would be removed when their present 'interim contract' came to an end. (It had actually run out two months earlier.) An appeal against the decision had to be launched, diverting time and energy away from the charity's core work looking after the young people themselves, and creating enormous stress and anxiety. And yet again the charity had to turn to its Christian supporters; an extra £1.25 a week from everyone who received the bulletin would replace the Supporting People funding, but it was too much to ask, especially of the many who were already giving more than they could really afford. As Peter said:

> The Lord has never failed us, though we have often failed him. You who have been supporting us for many years will have shared something of the remarkable ways in which the Lord has met our needs, but more often than not the deeply moving and often sacrificial giving of our prayer partners has met those needs. Your generosity has made us deeply aware of how carefully we must steward every gift we have received, and how highly we should value every item, every piece of equipment, tool, implement or vehicle that we have. All are gifts from the Lord, but nearly always through his own people.

Much of the burden of demonstrating the charity's viability fell on Simon Bryan Smith, who had taken up the post of

Caring For Life's accountant at the beginning of 2005. As he had soon discovered, this was a world away from accounting in the commercial world. 'I am beginning to learn to account by faith,' he said after three months in the job:

> Faith that there will be enough money to fix the minibus, pay the electricity bills or salaries. Maybe like me you have heard many talks concerning God's promises, and having the faith that he will provide, but never before have I been in the reality of standing on these promises in quite the same way as I do now!

Learning about the visions and plans for the future made him positively anxious when he was wearing his accountant's hat: his faith, he said, was not always sufficient to remove the uneasiness:

> Questions pop up in my head. But how much will that cost? Where will the money come from? What about the additional running costs? These are all helpful questions to ask, and ones I am employed to ask, but they have to be asked in light of a more important question: 'What does God want us to do?' This is not a question you will find in any accountancy textbook . . . Our challenge is to use good business practice and solid accountancy to fulfil God's plans.

Backed by Esther, Florence Hendriksz (the executive director) and a representative from the auditors, Simon held a meeting with the Supporting People team's head of finance and, as a result, Caring For Life received a certificate of accreditation. By the beginning of September 2006, Peter was able to report that the charity was 'moving towards' having a contract in place. Four years after the 'go live' date set for implementing the programme, Caring For Life finally received a three-year contract for Supporting People funding towards the cost of running the two homes and the Floating Support Project.

Undeterred by these problems, Caring For Life remains committed to the expansion and improvement of its services. As the twentieth anniversary of its foundation approaches, a new campaign has been launched to raise a substantial sum of money to build a new Adult Learning Centre at Crag House Farm. This would relieve pressure on the small Resource Centre, where literacy and numeracy lessons currently have to contend for space with art and craft, music, drama and catering academy classes, and all have to vacate the premises at mealtimes. The new centre would not only provide a better and safer environment for all these activities to take place but would also enable their quality to be improved. A library available to all those coming to the farm would also be included in the scheme, providing an important new resource for the 90% of those looked after by Caring For Life who suffer from poor reading skills. Up to 50% of the proceeds of each copy sold of this book will go towards the new centre.

In seeking donations, the charity has been hugely encouraged by the fact that one of Caring For Life's most generous supporters has offered to match any money raised up to the sum of £250,000. This magnificent offer was made at a fund-raising dinner, suggested and hosted by the charity's patron, HRH The Countess of Wessex, which raised the further sum of almost £35,000 towards the new centre.

Twenty years ago, four tragic young men had been gathered up into the loving arms of Caring For Life and given the promise that they would indeed be looked after for life. In that time, their lives have been changed beyond all recognition. Today, Colin is in a specialist provision where his serious psychotic condition is well cared for, but he still visits his friends at Caring For Life occasionally. Gary lives in Tindall House, has many friends, is a member of a local church, and enjoys a much happier relationship with his family. William lives in his own accommodation, has a small circle of friends, and has occasional employment. Owen, until recently, lived in his own flat with a partner and, having learnt to read and write at Caring For Life, now works as an assistant warehouse manager in a large store in Leeds. Owen's story, though apparently the most successful, has a poignant coda that is a lesson to all those who believe that two years is a sufficient period to provide support. Almost 20 years to the month since he first came to Caring For Life, he returned in despair. His relationship had broken down, he had had to leave the flat he shared with his partner and he had nowhere else to go. Just as it had done all those years ago, Caring For Life found him a new home, helped him to move in, and gave him the support he needed to continue with his job and his life.

Twenty years ago, the small band of remarkable people who founded Caring For Life had hoped that they could do something, no matter how small, to make a difference. They had recognized that the Dickensian underworld of the outwardly prosperous and supposedly morally upright Victorian era continued to flourish in the infinitely more wealthy and supposedly more socially conscientious twentieth century. Twenty years later nothing has changed. The poverty, the crime, the addiction, the violence, the abuse, the rejection, are all as rife in the twenty-first century as they were in the nineteenth. The bruises on the bodies and souls of yet another lost generation are just as livid today as they were in the past.

In the face of such overwhelming problems and insuperable need it is easier to close our eyes, shut our ears, and pretend that they do not exist. Yet the deafening sound of silent tears cannot be ignored. It cries out for comfort, for healing. Caring For Life takes the love of God into loveless places. More than 3,000 people have been found permanent homes and given hope for the future: more importantly, through their contact with the dedicated staff and volunteers who are the charity's life-blood, they have experienced the same unconditional love that Christ himself showed to mankind in a sinful world. Governments come and go; social policies change; but the love of Christ goes on for ever. The challenge to live the gospel remains.

'It seems miraculous to me that we are still here!' Peter wrote for the twentieth anniversary bulletin:

... but through many trials, many dangers, in spite of numerous mistakes on our part, by the Grace of God we are still here and still sharing the love of Jesus with any-

175

one who comes within the parameters of our care or who comes, for whatever reason, to visit us here at Crag House Farm.

As we try to take on board the huge challenges of the future, our task remains unchanged: for ours is the task that has belonged to every Christian and every church of every generation. It is very simply this: 'To share the love of Jesus' with as many people as we are able; to be faithful to Him and to try with all our being to simply be like Him; to love as He loves; to care as He cares. Oh, how we have failed Him, but we must embrace that vision and march on for His glory.

BC	6/12